PRAYERS

AND

SPIRITUAL FORMULAS

Copyright ©
Universal Brotherhood of Light

Prepared for print and new translation by Darin Stoytchev

Edited by Joel Mueller

Published August 2015

ISBN 978-1517076429

E-mail address: mainpem@gmail.com

Printed in Los Angeles, CA U.S.A

FOREWORD

This book is a collection of prayers given by the Master Beinsa Duno (or Douno)/Peter Dunov and some unknown brothers and sisters. Included are also spiritual thoughts- formulas which I believe are all by the master. Most of the translations of the prayers and formulas are my version of translation. Different translation variations are available on different web sites. There are some prayers and formulas that I have collected from lectures given by the Master. This book is available for free (digital format) together with two others "Love Wisdom Truth" and "The Might of Love" both by Beinsa Duno/Peter Dunov which I have translated. In my opinion all three are must read books for those who are searching for Divine Love, Wisdom, and Truth. Let us help one another by sharing them freely with all those who are seeking spiritual development and perfection. A few words about what Beinsa Duno preaches. I have been studying the lectures of the master Beinsa Duno for over 22 years and can wholeheartedly say that Beinsa Duno preaches a teaching of Love, Wisdom, and Truth. A teaching of brotherhood and sisterhood among all people. This teaching is not a sect, but open to each and everyone for studying. One can only benefit from studying and applying it. You are welcome to check it out for yourself.

Enjoy your reading.

To receive copies of the e-books send me an email at: mainpem@gmail.com

Darin Stoytchev

The Master Beinsa Duno About Prayer
(excerpts from lectures)

Remember the following truth. **There is no greater thing in Life than prayer.**

Prayer- this is a communication with God.

Prayer- this is an inner experience, inner connection with God. Pray, so you can be in connection with God.

No knowledge, no love, no wisdom in the world can be compared to prayer, to a person's communion with the Primary Principle.

There is no greater moment than that when one raises one's eyes towards God.

To pray means to direct one's mind, heart, soul and spirit towards the Great Source of Life from which we have emerged.

Prayer is a conversation of the soul with God, in which people confess their mistakes, rectify themselves and give thanks for all good things which they receive every day.

To pray means to send your report about the work you have done to That Center from which you have emerged.

In reply you will receive peace and enlightenment.

True prayer means the awakening of the Divine within the human being.

It concentrates human thinking, human feeling and human will in a single whole.

Such prayer is mighty; it can accomplish miracles.

If you persevere in prayer, you will always be joyful and happy; you will feel the Presence of God and will see that the Lord is true.

Prayers made with love are always received.

You will know that your prayer is received by that quiet joy, by that inner light, which will help you in resolving various tasks.

If you do not succeed in your prayer, you may seek the help of one, two or three persons, depending on the need.

Whoever prays from the bottom of their heart will invariably receive an answer!

Without prayer a person cannot make progress and learn.

Everything, which is done without prayer is difficult for the human spirit.

Knowledge or love or food without prayer is tedious to people.

Just as breathing is necessary for the body, so is prayer necessary for the soul.

Prayer is the most sacred action – the sole prerogative of the soul.

Prayer is not subject to any rule or limitation. If you pray correctly, you are always turned to God; no other image should exist in your mind.

Prayer is a conscious process of the human soul; it is the inner spiritual food of the soul; so it has a magical power.

When a person prays, they activate all their virtues simultaneously: Love, Wisdom, Truth, Justice, Compassion, Goodness and many other virtues.

Prayer is a Divine impulse. When it comes to you, you should not delay, but enter the secret chamber of your heart and start praying.

Prayer is an initiation to Divine life; prayer brings bliss.

Prayer is a method for resolving the three most difficult human tasks:
- to know yourself,
- to know your neighbor, and
- to know God.

All our works will be successful, if we begin with prayer.

We can pray at any time and in every circumstance because prayer relates to all spheres and moments of life.

Prayer has the power to heal any infirmities and illnesses, to purify one's mind and heart.

Pray to be liberated from all impurities, which tarnish you!

Prayer is even stronger when people undergo the greatest suffering and hardship.

In all circumstances prayer has the power to help!

Prayer is one of the best methods to refresh a man's mind and feelings. Prayer must be directed into connecting a man's soul with God. You will have an experience when you pray. And if you only come a few times in contact with God, you will receive incalculable riches.

Without prayer man cannot progress.

Christ Himself prayed. He had a great deal of knowledge, but every evening He was isolating Himself to pray and reason. If He had the need to pray, how much more should you!

Man can pray everywhere. You could be at a banquet, among friends and still be at prayer; there still will be a small gap during which you can pray. He, who knows, will find this gap and send his prayer. This is what it means to use our time consciously! I wish, you could constantly pray, i.e. in these gaps to be in connection with God. Thus only, upon you will come that effect from above. Then you will feel that Divine ennobling and strengthening.

Prayer must be directed at this- to connect one with God.

There is no nicer poetry in life than to pray, i.e. to have a conversation with God. Pray without complaining.

The best exercise in a man's life is prayer. For now, in the world, there is no nicer exercise than prayer.

Pray not only for yourself, but for all. He who thinks only of himself will achieve nothing. Pray before evil has come, before the bandits have attacked you, before a sickness has come on you. Pray before the mishap has come on you. In prayer you must be consistent 'till you lose your disposition, which shows, that your prayer, one way or another has been answered, positively or negatively it is answered. But prayer must have a grateful character for all goods and blessings, which the Lord gives us.

We have to pray not only when we are in a tight corner, but constantly.

He who wants something from the Lord must promise something (in turn), to sacrifice something from himself and whatever promises, he must fulfill.

The scripture says: **"Be constantly in prayer!"**

Prayer is the most beautiful thing in life.

In all conditions of life, in joy and sorrow, we should think of God.

We always need to pray!

Each one of you is preparing to become a citizen of the Kingdom of God, for which you should have the correct attitude towards God, towards your own soul and towards your neighbors. But you cannot establish these correct attitudes until you have a main idea within yourself.

You should concentrate all of your forces on one goal – to develop the Divine in yourself and to give it precedence over the human.

Value the Divine within yourselves – your mind, your heart, your soul and your spirit.

Learn to love your soul and you will be of help to yourselves.

The more you believe in your own internal forces and possibilities, the more rapidly you will develop.

"When I pray, "The Good Prayer" it takes me 15 minutes, the 91st PSALM – 20 minutes, "The Path of Life" – also 20 minutes. When I read "The Lord's Prayer", it takes me half an hour and when I get to the "Prayer of the Kingdom" it takes me another half an hour.

If you are in a hurry when you pray, nothing will be achieved.

15 minutes represent the law, by means of which all misunderstandings are dispelled,

20 minutes is the law of creation and work, 30 minutes is the law of equilibrium.

Whoever does not understand these laws will be discouraged, while whoever understands them will use the 15, 20 and 30 minutes in prayer and in reading the Bible."

Think about God, so you can become perfect like Him.

Think about God, so you can become good like Him.

Think about God, so you can become kind like Him.

Christ teaches: "Watch and pray so that you will not fall into temptation."

The Lord Jesus Christ

THE LORD JESUS CHRIST is Salvation and Hope for the world.

This thought is consoling for all those who believe in Him.

PRAYERS

*When you say **the Lord's Prayer**, give the following meaning to the words: Our Father, Who are in our minds, may Your Light come to my mind, so that it will be able to perceive. May Your Will be within all my undertakings, in all my thoughts and feelings, in all my actions. May Your Will be present even in my breathing and in my blood circulation, so that I can serve You in Joy and Love. 'Lead us not into temptation' means: Lord, give us knowledge and wisdom, so that we do not fall into temptation through our ignorance. ('Sacred Words of the Master', p.65)*

The Lord's Prayer
(New International Version)

Our Father in Heaven,
Hallowed be Your name. Your kingdom come. Your Will be done – on Earth as it is in heaven. Give us this day our daily bread.
And forgive us our debts, as we forgive our debtors. Lead us not into temptation, but deliver us from evil. For Yours is the kingdom, the Power and the Glory, forever.
Amen.

About **"The Good Prayer".**

"The Good Prayer" was given by the Master Beinsa Duno in 1900.

"The Good Prayer" is a password. You can pass everywhere by reading it. When you say "Lord, our God", you will go through the first door. You will pass through as many doors as there are sentences in it. The Good Prayer is sacred, as originating from God; and the Spirit of God vivifies it every day. Thus it is daily up-dated and never gets old. You shall read the Good Prayer in deep inspiration. You shall call the presence of the Spirit by your praying; you shall be very serene and master your mind. In this way you will form and send out that mighty force, those waves, which will attract the Power of God and will activate the Spirit. Then everyone will receive that gentleness and joy which you seek.

"Prayers and directions of the Master", 1925.

The Good Prayer

Lord, our God, our kind Heavenly Father, Who has given us life and health to rejoice in You, we pray to You, send us Your Spirit to guard and protect us from every evil and cunning thought.

Teach us to do Your Will, to sanctify Your Name and to glorify You always.

Illuminate our spirit, enlighten our hearts and our mind, that we may keep Your commandments and precepts.

With Your Presence, inspire Your Pure thoughts within us, and guide us to serve You with joy.

Our life, which we dedicate to You for the good of our brothers and neighbors, bless You Lord.
Help us and support us to grow in *all* knowledge and wisdom, to learn from Your Word and abide in Your Truth.

Lead us in everything we think and do in Your Name, that it may be for the victorious-success of Your Kingdom on Earth.

Nourish our souls with Your Heavenly bread, and strengthen us with Your Power, so that we may succeed in our life.

As You give us all Your blessings, so add unto us Your Love, to be our eternal law.

For to You belongs the Kingdom, the Power, and the Glory forever and ever.
Amen.

The Good Prayer and Psalm 91 used together attain such a great spiritual force that they can even save one's life in death strains.
They were recommended by the Master to some of the soldiers who were sent to the fronts during the Second World War.

Psalm 91 (New International Version)

1 He who dwells in the shelter of the Most High will rest in the shadow of the Almighty. **2** I will say of the LORD, "He is my refuge and my fortress, my God, in whom I trust." **3** Surely he will save you from the fowler's snare and from the deadly pestilence. **4** He will cover you with his feathers, and under his wings you will find refuge; his faithfulness will be your shield and rampart. **5** You will not fear the terror of night, nor the arrow that flies by day, **6** nor the pestilence that stalks in the darkness, nor the plague that destroys at midday. **7** A thousand may fall at your side, ten thousand at your right hand, but it will not come near you. **8** You will only observe with your eyes and see the punishment of the wicked. **9** If you make the Most High your dwelling-- even the LORD, who is my refuge-- **10** then no harm will befall you, no disaster will come near your tent.

11 For he will command his angels concerning you to guard you in all your ways; **12** they will lift you up in their hands, so that you will not strike your foot against a stone. **13** You will tread upon the lion and the cobra; you will trample the great lion and the serpent. **14** "Because he loves me," says the LORD, "I will rescue him; I will protect him, for he acknowledges my name. **15** He will call upon me, and I will answer him; I will be with him in trouble, I will deliver him and honor him. **16** With long life will I satisfy him and show him my salvation."

Prayer the Path of Life

Lord God, our Savior, of all Power and Might, of all Truth and Love, of all statehood and authority, wellspring of all goodness in life,
send us Your Kind Spirit to guide and support us on the Path of Life, to

enlighten our minds, to illuminate our hearts and to give us strength and vitality, so that we may do Your Kind Will.

Forgive us our transgressions, which we confess before You – they have moved us away from Your Fatherly Love. Efface them from the book of Your recollections, and grant us the peace of Your Spirit.

Let Your Face shine upon us now, so that we may become images of Your Love, messengers of Your Truth and servants of Your Justice.

Bless the nation within which we live. Bless our brothers and sisters with whom we work. Bless all mothers and fathers who do Your Will. Hear the voices of all who are suffering on the face of the Earth and bless them.

Bless our Master, Who is leading us in Your Path. Blessed are You, Lord our God.

Blessed is Your Name from ages past, for You are the Way, the Truth and Life and there is no other God, but You. You are the only One.

Amen.

Prayer of the Spirit

Lord our God, may Your Kind Spirit come and envelop our spirits in His Arms.

May It fill our hearts with the Boundless Love that reveals Your presence everywhere,

May It strengthen our hands in every righteousness and our feet in every goodness.

We bow before You, our Eternal Father, rock of our life.

Blessed are You, blessed is Your Name in our souls.

Strengthen us, uplift us, so that we may begin with *every joy* our serving for the coming of Your Kingdom, for the sake of your Love, which You have made manifest to us.

You are the only One, Who knows us and Whom we know – for You are the Light for our souls, expanse for our minds, increase to our power, fortress for our spirits, and fullness to our hearts.

You are the crown and glory of our life. Amen.

About "The Payer of the Spirit". When you read this Prayer, you should be very careful. Do not hurry, but concentrate your mind. Begin from the heart; put your heart and your mind in their places. Direct them to God and pronounce this Prayer.

(We read the Prayer of the Spirit for the first time kneeling on our right legs and lifting our right hands.) We need to think that all said in the Prayer will come true and will be fulfilled in our souls. (We read the Prayer once more, but this time with lifted left hands.)

Now we will kneel and will direct our minds to the Lord of Love with the following words:

Lord,
We are ready to fulfill Your Sacred Will absolutely, and without any changes. And our whole joy will be in serving You with all our hearts, minds, souls and spirits. We wish to know You as Love in us and outside us.

May You be all and everything in our beginnings, thoughts, desires and actions; may You be the beginning and the end of our life, the beginning of all Your Kindness and the end of all our misunderstandings; the beginning of Truth and the end of falsehood; the beginning of Wisdom and the end of foolishness; the beginning of Strength and the end of violence.

May You be a new beginning which has no beginning and no end. The beginning of the New Light, of the New Life. Come down to our souls, introduce Your Light of the New Life. Illuminate our new hearts which You have given us. Fill our minds with Your Light You have brought into our spirits. Bless us and we will carry Your Blessing."

Only those of you, who are willing to give promise, should use this part of the Prayer. ("Lectures, explanations and directions, given by the Master Beinsa Duno to the disciples of the Universal Brotherhood of Light at their meeting in the city of Veliko Turnovo in the summer of 1922." It was the year of the opening of the Divine School.)

Prayer of the Holy Spirit

Lord my God, my soul relies in You. Hear my supplication and give heed to my prayer. Uplift my spirit and give comfort to my heart. Show me the light of Your Face.

Lord, for the sake of Your Mercy, support me with the presence of Your Holy Spirit.

Lord, may Your Kingdom come, Your Justice be fulfilled, Your Truth beam out, Your Love be established and You, Lord Jesus Christ, the Only-Begotten Son of the Living God, dwell in Your fullness within my soul.

And may there be Glory to the Lord God, the Father, manifested in the Spirit of His Word throughout the ages.
Amen.

Prayer of the Kingdom

This prayer was given by the Master Beinsa Douno at the annual meeting of the Spiritual Circle on August 16, 1909 – Sunday

Lord our God, may our prayer rise up before Your Face. May Your Spirit come and may Your Word abide in our hearts, for the sake of Your Love – which you are bestowing upon us.

Kind Heavenly Father, Abba, Father, may Your Kingdom come, may Your will be done, may Your Name be sanctified on Earth, this is what our souls desire. This is the need, which we constantly feel in this world.

Great Lord of all power and every fortress, stand behind Your Deed, inspire the hearts of all those whom You have chosen to be called the commencement of Your glory and greatness.

Our kind Lord, lead us with Your merciful hand, enlighten us, so that we do stray from Your Word and we do not transgress Your Law.

Lead us like a good shepherd to the green pastures and clear springs.

You, One Lord and Savior of the world, known before all the ages of light, One in the beaming light of our lives – deign to expand my soul, uplift our spirit, renew our hearts, enlighten our minds, so that we may glorify You now and always.
Amen.

Prayer the Fruits of the Spirit

Lord of lovingness, God of Love – we call upon You in Your Mercy. We accept the sufferings, which You send us with joy in our heart. We accept the difficulties, which You give to us for the strengthening of our spirit. We will fulfill Your Kind Will without hesitating or vacillating.

Send us Your Spirit to bring into our hearts, our minds and our souls the fruit of Your Love, the goodness of Joy and Peace, the Foundation of Your Patience and Compassion.

Grant us the Gift of Faith, Humility and Temperance.

Bless us as You have always blessed us. Make Your Name dear to our souls. Establish Your Kingdom in our souls. Nourish our souls with Your Word that all Your virtues may be fortified in us. May

Your Radiant Spirits of Love, Faith and Hope abide within us now and forever together with You.

We bring You praise, glory be to You, the One Lord and God of the Great Sacrifice.
Amen.

Prayer of the Triune God

1. Lord, may Your Kind Spirit come upon my spirit – to fill my heart and soul with Your presence, and to strengthen my feet in every righteousness.

I bow before the Eternal Rock out of which I have been carved. Blessed is Your Name, Lord.

Strengthen me and uplift me that I may serve You with gladness.

2. Lord, my God, may Your Spirit come and enlighten my mind, illuminate my heart and fill my soul with every joy and gladness.

I bow before You, the Eternal Wellspring Who has always watered me. Wash my feet and cleanse my heart, bleach my soul so that I may be pure and sacred before You.

Blessed are You, Lord, my God!

3. Lord, my God, may Your Blessing come upon my spirit, to fill my heart and my soul with the good fruits of Your Spirit, to make my feet firm with the strength of Your presence.

I bow before Your Eternal Spirit Who vivifies me and resurrects me from the dead.

Protect me, Lord, with Your Sacred Name, and strengthen me so I can serve You with joy and gladness and be one with You, Lord Jesus Christ as You are One with the Father.
Amen.

Prayer of Sacred Purity

Lord, our God, of all inner fullness of life, we stand before Your face, according to Your Great Mercy, which brings the light of Your face, a gift for our souls.

We have purified our mouths and Your glory filled our speech. We glorify You, we praise You. Your Kind Spirit has cleansed our hearts and we sing praise to Your name and receive the great joy, which it brings into our life.

Your Great Spirit has cleansed our minds and in us was born an irresistible inner desire to work for the Glory of Your Holy Name and to spread Your Great

Thoughts throughout the whole world. You have purified our souls and in us arose the sacred desire of eternity, in which You dwell, to work for the good of our neighbors and for the good of our souls.

For the sake of Your Mercy, which dwells only in You,

bless us,
illuminate us,
uplift us,
strengthen us,
resurrect us

and fill our souls with Your Kind Spirit, so that we may always serve You with joy and gladness. May we carry the image of Your Love, the Light of Your Truth, the consonance of Your Wisdom, the Foundation of Your Goodness and the Purity of Your Justice.

Amen.

The Small Prayer

Lord, my God-
make me so that I can see Your
Face. Gladden me for the sake of Your
Name. Bless me for the sake of Your
Mercy.
Enlighten me for the sake of Your Spirit.
Uplift me for the sake of Your Word.
Help me for the sake of Your Promise.
Guide me for the sake of Your Truth.
Support me for the sake of Your Justice.
And blessed be You, Lord, always,
because You are Kind and Truthful
towards all.
Amen.

Prayer of Gratitude

I thank You, our Father, for the Great
Love with which You have loved us. I
thank You for the life which You have
given us. I thank You for the mind which

you have put in us. I thank You for the Virtues which You have placed as a foundation of our lives. I thank You for the Justice with which You have surrounded us. I thank You for the Love with which You have filled us. I thank You for Your Great Wisdom and we glorify You for Your Truth with which You have enlightened us. We rejoice in the Life which You have given us and we fulfill Your Will. Now, for the sake of the Spirit Whom You have sent to lead us, make sooner the awakening of the consciousness, so Your Kingdom be established on Earth, and all men give songs of praise to Your Greatness and Your Throne. Be blessed by all of us, now and always.

Amen.

(Given at the first supper in the city of Varna (Bulgaria) on 08/19/1903. Then the Master turned to his three disciples- Dr. Mirkovitch, Penu Kirov, and Todor

Simenov and told them: "Now you are three, but you will become many.")

Prayer of the Chosen Ones

Lord, bless this nation, strengthen it, raise it, give it bravery. Wing its spirit, give it faith, trust, hope in You to awaken and glorify You throughout all future ages.

Accomplish this, Lord, our God, because of Your Great Name, by which You have been known throughout all ages.

Make Your Name to shine before all nations and may they know that You are the only One, in Whom there is no change and Who is always strong to help and save.

Disperse our enemies, Lord, from in front of Your Face and we will glorify You with a pure heart, when You help us to get over the cunning spirits of hell, who want to spoil Your holy Work.

You, Lord, alone do act now with Your strong Hand. Accomplish this for our Lord Jesus Christ, through Whose Name You have blessed us to call upon You.
Amen.

Blessing the Bulgarian Nation
(You can put the name of the country of your choice.)

Lord, God of Powers,
In the Name of Christ, through Which Name You have deigned to call You, we, Your children are coming this morning to kneel before You. Our appeal, Lord, is to bless and guard the Bulgarian nation, its sacred circle, the priests, the ministers, the farmers, the teachers, the traders, the workers of noble labor, all mothers and fathers who fulfill Your Will and all good persons who work for the coming of Your Kingdom on Earth. May You extend Your Right Hand upon them and stroke them.

Lord, raise Your Face above them and give them Peace! Bless the Bulgarian nation in order to overcome all guiles of the evil one and all his dark forces.

We ask You, bless the soul and the spirit of this nation, so that it can glorify You throughout the future centuries.

Amen.

The New Credo

I believe in the One Eternal True God Who has spoken to me in the past, Who speaks to me in the present, and Who will speak to me in the future.

I believe in the Lord and His Spirit, Who created the conditions for my salvation.

I believe in the Lord Jesus Christ, Who came to save the world.

Amen.

Prayer for Personal Uplifting

Lord, teach me to love You thus, as You love me.
Amen.

Prayer my Belief

I believe in You, Lord, Who has spoken to me in the past.
I believe in You, Lord, Who speaks to me now.
I believe in You, Lord, Who will speak to me in the future.
May Your Name be glorified, and may we live in Your Glory.
May Your Kingdom be established, and may we partake in Your Joy.
May Your Will be done on Earth, as it is in Heaven, and may we work together with You.
Amen – So Be It!

Prayer for Full Success of the Cause

Lord, illuminate the whole of humanity in the Spiritual Chain with Your Light and Power. May the whole of humanity accept Christ Teachings!

May all come to believe that You exist!

May the idea for God grow up in all souls! Those, who preach godlessness, may they become successors of Your Word, and may all non-believers become believers!

Lord, we zealously entreat You, Your Divine Mercy to inundate the whole Earth, and Your Divine Love to fill all hearts.

Lord, illuminate with Your Light all nations and their leaders, so they become harmonized and come to an agreement on all issues, so that Your Peace be established on Earth.

Lord, may fraternization come among all nations on the face of the Earth.

Lord, bring in life, light and uplift in all study groups of the Universal Brotherhood of Light in the whole world.
Amen.

Praise to the King of All Ages

Lord our God, Our souls quietly trust in You. You have revealed Your Paths to us and we see Your Kindness. You have manifested Your Mercy to us and we see Your Long-suffering. You have shown Your Love to us and we see Your Goodness. You have pointed the Truth to us and we see Your Holiness. You have made Your Name known to us and we see Your Justice. You have revealed Your Wisdom to us and we see Your great deeds. You have turned our hearts and we see Your Presence everywhere. You have enlightened our minds and we see Your Creations, that all of them are good. You have surrounded us with Your Strength and we know Your might.

And after all goods and blessings which You have poured down upon us, according to Your inner fullness, our desire is always to see Your Face and to rejoice and be pleased in the fullness of Your Love.

We thank You for Your care with which You have surrounded us. We thank You that Your Mercy and Kindness always follow us. We thank You that You have always listened to us and have always been ready to give us help and to support us when we are in need.

Kindly Lord, Holy Father of Heaven and Earth, deliver us from the wiles of the cunning one. Here You have spoken to us and we believe that You will affirm us throughout all ages so as to glorify You.

Lord, our God, Who is changeless, support our weak brothers and sisters so that they may dwell in You and You may dwell in them, as You dwell in me, so that we may all be one – as You are with me, so am I in them so that we may become one to glorify You on Earth with the fruits which we will bear in justice and mercy – so that our deeds are enlightened before people and after seeing them, they will glorify You.

    Kindly Father, You Who gives us life and health, Who provides us with bread and water and Who satisfies us through the thousands of Your blessings every day, Your Sun rises every morning like a bridegroom and runs in its path which You have ordained, giving Your blessings, which You have prepared for us. In Your Name it enlivens the whole Earth and Nature, uplifts and brings the clouds, waters its face with rain and moisture, brings out every stalk from beneath the black cover of the ground, decorates the wild flowers with all their beauty that You have initially given them. It gladdens all animals and humans whom You have made in Your image and after Your likeness. It inspires hope and faith in their hearts, so that they may labor and work, while telling them that You will bless their labor.

How many are Your ordinances! They all cannot be numbered.

We, all Your children, come today to bring You our gratitude, that You have dressed us in the clothes of life. And how beautiful are these clothes with which You have enveloped us.

Blessed Lord, blessed from all ages, receive now our grateful supplication.

Amen.

Prayer of Daniel
(2:19)

19 Then was the secret revealed unto Daniel in a vision of the night. Then Daniel blessed the God of heaven. 20 Daniel answered and said:

"Blessed be the name of God forever and ever; for Wisdom and Might are His.

21 He changes times and seasons;
He removes kings and sets up kings;
He gives wisdom to the wise
and knowledge to those who have understanding;
22 He reveals deep and hidden things;
He knows what is in the darkness,
and the light dwells with Him.
23 To You, God of my fathers,
I give thanks and praise, for You have given me wisdom and might, and have now made known to me what we asked of You, for You have made known to us the king's matter.
 Amen.

Prayer when in difficulty

Lord, You are the One Who can set everything right. You arrange things the best.
 Amen.

Prayer

Turn to God with the words:

Lord, we want to fulfill Your law, to do Your Will and to manifest Your thought. Amen.

Fulfill everything with gratefulness for the Love of God for you, and do not doubt in Him!

Let's direct our hearts toward Christ and thank Him for His love for us. To love means this is the fulfillment of Christ's law. When you fulfill that law, you are connecting yourself with God. What is there greater for one than that connection?

(From the lecture: "Whoever comes to me I will not drive away. 03/16/1924, Sofia, Bulgaria.)

Morning Prayers

Morning Prayer of the Disciple
(given in the city of Plovdiv, Bulgaria)

Lord our God, my soul quivers with joy before the Light of the new day, which dawns on me.

I thank You for awakening me early in the morning, when You are glorified by the wise, the birds and the pure flowers.

I thank You for giving me the gift of another day of life, and for calling me to pursue my work on Earth healthy and restored.

I thank You for giving me the chance to accomplish Your Good Will, to manifest it with Love and Wisdom, as I serve my brothers and sisters.

I plead with You, grant me the presence of Your Kind Spirit, that I may listen to Your guidance like a faithful child and that my soul may not divert from Your Law.

Give me strength, vigilance and love to live for my whole uplifting and that of all humans and all beings and for the coming of the Kingdom of God on Earth.

May the Eternal Sun of Your Love illuminate with its light my soul and those of all my brothers and sisters on the face of the Earth.

May Your Love, Wisdom, Truth, Justice and Virtues begin to reign in the life of man!

May all humans become One with Christ and the bright angels, one with You and The Great Brotherhood of Light!

Amen.

Morning Prayer

Lord, You have sent me to the Earth.
You have given me life and health.
You have given me heart, mind and soul
that I may do Your Will and glorify You.

I will do Your Will.
I will glorify You.
And after I fulfill God's Will and after God gives me His blessing, I will do what is good for my soul and will help those close to me.
Amen.

Morning Prayer

Lord, thank You, that I have remained alive so that I can serve You today too. Bless my soul, Lord! Thank You that I have remained today to do my work which I must do. Wherever I go, I can grow as much as needed.
Amen.

Morning Prayer

Lord, thank You, that I have remained alive so that I may serve You today too.

Bless my soul, Lord! Thank You that I have remained today to do my work which I must do. Wherever I go, I can grow as grow as much as needed.

Thank You, God for the great goodness, that You have for me. I know that You are Good, All-merciful, All-truthful and All-wise. Thank You, Lord for everything You have given me and taught me.

Amen.

Morning Prayer

Bless my soul, Lord! Thank you that I have risen today to finish my work as I should. Wherever I am, I can grow as much as needed.

Amen.

Morning Prayer
(prayer to have our things going well)

Every morning at awakening, put your hands on top of your head and tell yourself:

"Lord, I want to serve you with all of my mind, with all of my heart, with all of my soul and, with all of my spirit!
Amen."

(from the lecture "Under the Sun Rays" 08/27/1938 5 a.m.)

Morning Prayer

Bless, Lord, my soul. Cleanse me, God, from evil thoughts. I thank You for the Great Goodness which You have shown towards me. I know You as good, all-merciful, all-truthful and all-wise. Thank You, Lord, I thank You for everything You have given me and taught me.
Amen.

Morning Prayer

Thank You, Lord, for protecting me during last night. Help me not to commit any sin and help me spend this day doing Your Will.
Amen.

Prayer on Awakening

Lord, lead me towards Your Great Understanding, fortified by Your Good Will!
Lord, bless my brothers and sisters as You have blessed me.
I will serve You as You have taught me, I will spread Your Love according to Your Will.
I thank You, Lord, for every good, which You have given me and taught me.
I thank You, Master, that You have preserved my life and health today as always!
Amen.

Evening Prayer
(concentration at 10:00 pm.)

Lord, we thank You for the beautiful life, for this beautiful world, which You have created for us. We want to live according to this Love, which You have put in our souls. May Your Light illuminate our minds. May with that Light we solve the Divine issue which lies before the door of our soul.
Amen.

Evening Prayer
(to be said at bedtime)

Lord, during the time of my sleep tonight, envelope me with Your Light and protect me, for I go Beyond, to study, to pray and to work.
I want to meet with Christ and I believe that this will happen, because this is His Will, and His Will can not be broken.
Amen.

Evening Prayer

Kind Lord, this evening I want to go to the School, the School of The Universal Brotherhood of Light. The Lord loves me, and I love Him. He is boundless and that is why he loves me. And there is absolutely no doubt in His Love. I will be up, because the Lord has said so, His word cannot be split in two.
Amen.

Evening Prayer

God of Power, send Your Holy Spirit to illuminate my room with Your Light and with the Power of Your Spirit, surround my bed with the fiery circle of Your Love that my room and all of my house may be free from every evil influence.

Perfection in Your Love will be the meaning of my life.

Your perfect Love casts out every fear from my soul and brings peace and joy to my spirit.
Amen.

Prayer for Every Day

Lord, enlighten my mind, bless my heart, strengthen my will, my memory and my faith so as to justify my existence and to solve the task for which I have come on Earth.

Lord, please send Your Spirit to bring into my heart, into my mind and my soul the fruit of Love, the good of Joy and Peace – the foundation of Your Patience and Mercy.
Amen.

Prayer for Protection in Thunderstorms and Earthquakes

Everything which is good I accept.
Whenever I want to do something good, there is no power, that can prevent me.
I can do everything through the living Lord of Love, Who has created everything in the world.
Amen.

(The Master has said: "This is my greeting for December 17, when Christ comes and you should greet Him like that. When you begin to hear the thunders, when the ground under your feet begins to dance, say the above thoughts and have no fear. Let those thoughts remain in you when needed.")

Prayer for Rain

Lord, if it is Your Will, according to Your Love, forgive the transgressions of the whole humanity and give rain on the face of the whole Earth!
Amen.

(This prayer seems to be a general prayer for rain. I think we could specify the geographical area where we want to rain.)

*About the **"Prayer of the Spirit of the Solid Foundation"**.*
In a letter dated 22.11.1913 the Master wrote the following about the Prayer of the Spirit of the Solid Foundation:
"Five things are needed in a man's life:
*Healthy body
*Good heart
*Bright mind
*Strong/Mighty soul

*Robust spirit

I wrote you a prayer so that you may have a form; allow your spirit to work upon it, multiply and propagate it. Go deep into the core of its meaning. I wish you to be free from all affectations in life. I point out to you five things which to develop and to acquire. Only then will you be one with Me. Keep this prayer as something valuable for you. These things are rarely given. Do not entrust it to anyone. May it be your wealth in the world. You may pray whenever you prefer. Keep the sanctified things; do not give them to the unworthy ones. Seek the power and the freedom of your spirit. May Christ, the One living word, be your joy and gladness forever."

Prayer of the Spirit of the Solid Foundation

Lord my God, my soul trusts in You. Hear my supplication and give heed to my prayer.

Uplift my spirit and give comfort to my heart.

Lord, show me the Light of Your face and for the sake of Your mercy support me with the presence of Your Holy Spirit.
Amen.

Prayer of the Disciples of the Brotherhood of Light

We thank You, Lord, that we have been born in this epoch.
We thank You that You have called and awakened us into the fold of the Brotherhood of Light.

We supplicate You, through the Power of Your Spirit, the Great Spirits of the Living God and our contact through Your Word, that those souls in the world who do not yet know You to awaken.

Bless all those who work for Your cause. Increase their number, so that they may work in the Divine Field for coming of the Kingdom of God on Earth.

Amen.

Prayer of the Disciple

I chose the Path of Truth!

I will walk in Your Truth! Teach me, Lord, and lead me in Your Way! Send me Your Light and Your Truth, so that they guide me! Give me faith! I have faith, Lord!

Amen.

Prayer of The Disciple

Lord, be always with us.
Teach us Your ways.
Take us under Your wing according to
Your mercy.
Protect us for Your Deed.
May God's Peace be upon all of us.
Amen.

Prayer of The Disciple

I beg You, for wisdom, my God!
Support me, give me Love. I will eternally
Love You. I will eternally serve You
Amen.

Prayer of The Disciple

Lord, be always with us. Teach us Your ways. Protect us according to Your mercy. Guard us for Your cause.
May God's Peace be upon us all.
Amen.

The Good Path
prayer of the disciple

Lord of Light, of all fullness and kindness,
about which my Master has spoken to me, reveal Yourself to me as You deign, as it is pleasing to You.

I am ready to fulfill Your Will without any deviation, without any hesitation, without any doubt. And I will be as faithful and truthful, Lord, as You are faithful and truthful. For the sake of the Name of my Master, through Whom You have spoken to me, may I always rejoice in the presence of Your Word, in the manifestation of Your Great and Sacred Spirit. And may I always be like the little children of Your Kingdom – obedient, diligent, constant, patient, content in Your Boundless Love, Which You show towards all the weak and powerless who seek the Path of Your Eternal Light, in which You dwell.

Please, Lord, enlighten me and let not the presence of Your Kind Spirit move away from my soul, from my heart, from my mind, from my will.

Lord, may I be a bearer of Your Word, a doer of Your Will; may I always do what is pleasing to You, what You want.

May Your Spirit dwell in my soul, may I rejoice in the presence of Your Light, for the sake of the Name of my Master, through which You are known in the world.
Amen.

Prayer to the Spirit of Truth

(the hands are raised up with open palms)
Concentrate your thought so that the Spirit of Truth begin to act and pronounce the following:

1. May God submit every lower act in us to the Spirit of Truth.
2. May God's Love, Wisdom, and Truth come to reign in all their fullness in our soul.
3. And so, we are opening our hearts for the Lord, Who is now among us. May His Name be glorified.

Amen.

The Beautiful Prayer
(prayer, given to a group of ten disciples)

Lord God, make us as firm as a diamond, so that we may become the foundation of the New Universe. Make us like pillars in Your Living Church, so that we may receive the Divine Life for the others.

Illuminate us with the Power of Your Holy Spirit, so that we may awaken the sleeping souls with the Word, Thought and Deed.

Reveal in us, Kind Lord, Your Divine Essence, help us to attain strength, so that we may know the Truth, that we may become children of Light, that we may walk in the Path of Justice, for the realization of Your Plan and for the coming of Your Kingdom on Earth.

Amen.

The most beautiful prayer is concluded in this, a man must think about God as a source of life.

The Master

Prayer in Sanskrit
(in Bulgarian)

Сарбе нато ихриш Версана. Версана нато херманит тукла бисмерто лебени. Салба михлер бада Силер, хлерманде ихбриш, Барманде Натан индерман.

Prayer in Sanskrit
(pronounce every sound)

Sarbe nato ihrish Versana. Versana nato hermanit tucla bismerto lebeni. Salba mihler bada Siler, hlermande ihbrish, Barmande Natan inderman.

Prayer for Healing

Lord, You are the Source of Life, send us Your life-giving power- the Spirit to heal my mind, heart, spirit, will and body. To heal me from all psychic and physical illnesses and sufferings. To gift me with

health, strength and life, with youth and beauty, and to develop in me gifts and abilities, so I can live, study and serve You.
Amen.

Prayer for Healing

Lord, help me in this hard hour to get rid of the illness, so I can serve You with joy. I want to dedicate my life in serving Love, in the fulfillment of Your Will.
Amen.

Prayer For Healing

Lord, You are the Source of Life, send us Your life-giving strength, Your Spirit to heal us from all illnesses and sufferings.
(3 times)
Amen.

Prayer for Health

When you get sick, have no fear, but put your hands on the place where the illness is and say:

And this is Eternal Life to know You, the One, the Only True God and Christ Whom You have sent.
This is Eternal Life to know Love, Wisdom and Truth.
This is Eternal Life to know that God is Spirit Who reigns everywhere.
Amen.

Prayer for 10 Day Fasting

Lord, accept me in the healing facility of Nature for ten days.

Prayer for Healing of Another Person

Ever-present and all-kind God, in the Name of the Lord Who has spoken to Your servant, let Your healing come through us, Your servants, for the glory of Your Name.

We thank You that You have heard us. Only You are our God and we have no other God but You.

It is You Who can always heal, and Your Healing is health for the soul and for the body.

Restore the harmonious activity between the mind and the soul, between the soul and the body.

Turn the fount of the heart to good and the forces of the body to purposeful work.

Let this our brother/sister .... (name) who is suffering receive Your mercy that we may all rejoice in the presence of Your Love, Kindness and Power.

(To be said on Wednesday, Saturday and Sunday at 7.00 a.m. and 9.00 a.m.)

Prayer for Healing of Another Person

Lord of the powers, You are our refuge from generation to generation. Your mercies we glorify forever. You have made covenant with Your chosen ones, because You have a sound and strong hand to give mercy to those, who know You in Your Name.

Turn, God, Your eyes to the suffering brother/sister .... (name), give heed to his/her sufferings and relieve them. We firmly believe in Your words, when you said: "Call to Me and I will answer you, because I am your God, Who supports your right hand and tells you: "Do not be afraid, I will help you! Do not be afraid, Because I chose you, I called you by name. You are not alone when you walk through the water, I will be with you when you walk through the fire, you will not be burned and the flame will not burn you. Do not be afraid when powerless, too, because I am with you!"

Now hear my prayer, God, pour over him/her of Your abundant mercy!
Amen.

Prayer Before and After Meals

God's Love brings the abundant and full life.
(3 times)

Prayer Before and After Meals

God's Love brings the abundant and full life.
Only God's Love brings the abundant and full life.
Only the manifested God's Love brings the abundant and full life.

Prayer Before Meal

(Variation II used in combination with the prayer after meal below)

God's Love brings the abundant and full life.
(3 times)

Prayer After Meal

Only the manifested God's Love brings the abundant and full life.
(3 times)

Prayer Before Meal

You are blessing us, Lord and we are receiving from the abundance of Your Kindness.
(3 times)

Prayer Before Meal

Thank You, Lord, for the bread, which You have given me. I want to be pure and stable like the wheat grain.
Amen.

Prayer Before Meal

Lord, thank You for the bread, which you have given me. Thank You for the life which You are putting in me through it.
Amen.

Lozinka
(Lozinka is a diminutive form of 'vine'- loza)

Lord, bless and strengthen our souls!
1. We pray to our Heavenly Father for glorifying and sanctifying the Name of the Lord – our God on Earth, among the

people, and the believers and among the elect from the Circle of the God of Glory – the Savior, the Protector, Who raises and resurrects the dead and puts law and order everywhere. And blessed be the Name of our Lord Jesus Christ – the Manifested Word of God and with Him all those who love Him.

2. We pray to our Heavenly Father for the coming of the Kingdom of God on Earth among the people, in the hearts of the believers and in the souls of the elect. And may every Justice, every Good, every Wisdom and every Truth be put into action. May the Lord our God come to reign and may the words of the Lord: "The Lord has deigned to give you a kingdom." be fulfilled.

And may the Spirit of our Lord Jesus Christ be instilled among us and may the primordial intention of our Father of Light and of the Bright, Radiant Spirits be fulfilled, and may there be Glory and

Honor, and adoration towards Him now, always and throughout all ages.

3. We pray to our Heavenly Father for the fulfillment of the Will of our Lord God on Earth, as it is in Heaven, among the Bright Angelic Faces. And may the Law of Truth, Love and Justice be established, so that we may be all in One body and One spirit. And may there be order, consonance and praise, may knowledge how to glorify Him be given to us; and may we all rejoice in the Lord and His Deeds. And may He be instilled in our life and in the Work of His Hands. And may He give life and health, and longevity to all those who trust in Him. And may He deliver them from all the deeds of evil and of the sly one. May He bring peace into their souls. May He give them abundance of His Kindness.

May the Lord our God remember His Promises, may He have mercy on all those who suffer. May He bless all believers. May He strengthen His elect, may He give them Strength, Knowledge, Wisdom and Love to prevail for Him in His Holy Name. May He give us victory over our enemies, to win to the end and to serve the Lord with joy and gladness throughout all the days of our life.

May He illuminate us with the Light of His Face and make us strong and firm, so that we may accomplish His Good Will. May we walk before Him in wisdom, without evil and with fullness. May He heal all our suffering brothers and sisters. May He bless their homes and also their children. May He bless all the good initiatives of their bodies, souls and spirits.

And thus may the Lord our God rise within us as He is in heaven.

Amen.

Lozinka

I wish, Lord, in all Your fullness to come Your peace in my heart and in the hearts of all, so we can bring peace and joy to all who suffer, to all those who wait for You, and are ready to do everything on Earth for Your Glory. Bless, Lord, our work which we are undertaking now to be for the glory of Your Name on earth. Let it be, Lord, as You have said: "Peace I leave with you, My peace I give you."

(We will pray to God to give us a way to be reasonable, to bring peace everywhere, as it is said in the Scripture: "Be at peace with all men!")

Come Your Light, Lord, and Your face shine upon us, as You have said, "I Am the Light of the world" thus may Your Word be a light for us, may our deeds shine before the world, so when men see them, glorify You.

(May we have the necessary light for each work. So we can know how to do a thing and be pleased with it, light is needed.)

Lord, may Your Mercy come upon us, because You have said that You are kind, merciful and good. And may we be like You, Lord, so that I and all know that You are merciful and Good Lord who saves everyone.

(If God's Mercy does not permeate our souls, we will not have mercy, we will not have the ease and will not be able to study and work. The Master)

May Your Word, Lord, be fulfilled as you have said: "Stay in Jerusalem, until you are filled with the Holy Spirit." We stand before Your face, Lord, and we entreat You, fill us with Your Bright Spirit, so we can bring the good news of Your Word to all who expect You.

Lord, because You have made man in Your image and likeness, we entreat You, support our souls so we can always keep this great good that You have given us, so we and all can always be healthy, and to glorify You together through all ages. We pray for the life and health, which You have given us, to use them for Your glory on earth.

(We'll have light upon the inner side of which lie the life and health).

Thank You, Lord, for all the good and all the beauty which You have place within us. We entreat You, support us to always keep this good and this beauty, as the most - precious for our soul, and they be the best - fragrance before Your Face, so that all this be in me, and in all, for Your Glory.

Prayers for The Departed

When we pray for the departed the order is:

1. Prayer for the departed.
2. Secret prayer
   (this is a prayer you create)
3. The Lords Prayer.
4. Psalm 23.
5. Psalm 121.
6. Prayer of Denial.

7. XIV Chapter from The Gospel of saint John.

8. The Formulas:

And this is Eternal Life to know You, the One, the Only True God and Christ Whom You have sent.

(three times)

Peace to his/her soul and Eternal Light to his/her path

(three times)

Prayer for the Departed Souls

Lord, rest the Soul of the departed brother/sister .... whom You have taken above according to Your Will. Accommodate him/her in luminous places in Your domicile. Grant him/her with Your Spiritual Virtues, so that he/she may uplift him/herself, revive him/herself and see Your Glory and Greatness. May his/her soul rejoice in Your Kindness and

Love. May eternal Peace and eternal Light reign upon his/her soul!
Amen.
(3 times)

Prayer for the Departed Souls

Lord, give light and peace to our beloved brother/sister .... Make straight his/her path by leading him/her to Yourself. Shed light on his/her path, send to him/her souls which will guide, teach and assist him/her on the path that leads him/her to You.

Lord, accept .... in Your Bosom. Enfold him/her with Your Boundless Love and lead him/her in the Light of Your Wisdom.

Lord, bless .... and let him/her advance from love to love, from light to light, from bliss to bliss, and from freedom to freedom.

Lord, bless .... Grant peace to his/her soul and eternal light to his/her path.
Amen.
(3 times)

Secret Prayer
(a prayer you create)

....
....

The Lord's Prayer

Our Father in Heaven,
Hallowed be Your name. Your kingdom come. Your Will be done – on Earth as it is in heaven. Give us this day our daily bread, and forgive us our debts, as we forgive our debtors. Lead us not into temptation, but deliver us from evil. For

Yours is the kingdom, the Power and the Glory, forever.
   Amen.

Psalm 23 (New International Version)

A psalm of David.
1 The LORD is my shepherd, I shall not be in want. 2 He makes me lie down in green pastures, he leads me beside quiet waters, 3 he restores my soul. He guides me in paths of righteousness for his name's sake. 4 Even though I walk through the valley of the shadow of death, I will fear no evil, for you are with me; your rod and your staff, they comfort me 5 You prepare a table before me in the presence of my enemies. You anoint my head with oil; my cup overflows. 6 Surely goodness and love will follow me all the days of my life, and I will dwell in the house of the LORD forever.

Psalm 121 (New International Version)

A song of ascents.
1 I lift up my eyes to the hills-- where does my help come from? 2 My help comes from the LORD, the Maker of heaven and earth. 3 He will not let your foot slip-- he who watches over you will not slumber; 4 indeed, he who watches over Israel will neither slumber nor sleep. 5 The LORD watches over you-- the LORD is your shade at your right hand; 6 the sun will not harm you by day, nor the moon by night. 7 The LORD will keep you from all harm-- he will watch over your life; 8 the LORD will watch over your coming and going both now and forevermore.

Prayer of Daniel
(2:19)

19 Then was the secret revealed unto Daniel in a vision of the night. Then Daniel blessed the God of heaven. 20 Daniel answered and said:
"Blessed be the name of God forever and ever; for Wisdom and Might are His.
21 He changes times and seasons;
He removes kings and sets up kings;
He gives wisdom to the wise
and knowledge to those who have understanding;
22 He reveals deep and hidden things;
He knows what is in the darkness,
and the light dwells with Him.
23 To You, God of my fathers,
I give thanks and praise, for You have given me wisdom and might, and have now made known to me what we asked of You, for You have made known to us the king's matter.
    Amen.

John 14:1-7 *(New International Version)*

14 "Do not let your hearts be troubled. You believe in God[a]; believe also in me. 2 My Father's house has many rooms; if that were not so, would I have told you that I am going there to prepare a place for you? 3 And if I go and prepare a place for you, I will come back and take you to be with me that you also may be where I am. 4 You know the way to the place where I am going."

5 Thomas said to him, "Lord, we don't know where you are going, so how can we know the way?"

6 Jesus answered, "I am the way and the truth and the life. No one comes to the Father except through me.

7 If you really know me, you will know[b] my Father as well. From now on, you do know Him and have seen Him."

Formulas

And this is Eternal Life to know You, the One, the Only True God and Christ Whom You have sent.
(3 times)

Peace to his/her soul and Eternal Light to his/her path
(3 times)

Prayer

I must be healthy as God requires. I must be good, as God requires. I must be strong as, God requires. I must be such, as God wants me to be.
Amen.

Prayer for Blessing
(of another person)

Lord, bless (name ....) to walk tirelessly in the path of Truth and Good, and all of his/her feelings, wishes, actions and deeds to be leavened from the living Truth, which comes out from the Spirit of Love.

Lord, give light to (name ....).

Lord, You, who lives in him/her, look benevolently towards him/her. Let him/her show Your Love and mercy, let him be a conductor of God's blessing and bliss!
Amen.

AGNUS DEI

This Prayer is from the black and white shepherd's plaid pocketbook of the Master, in which he noted his reflections in the period from 3.03.1899 up to 16.10.1900.

Lord Jesus, Agnus Dei,
May Your blessing be with me day and night.
Lord, You are my fullness. In You my soul will find the strength to stand. Without You life will perish, the spirit will be weakened.
Lord, my hope of any age in this waterless and desert land, in which my spirit is depressed, You said that living water would spring forth even in the desert for those who trust in You. Lord, I wish to see Your Face in this land, so that my spirit will rejoice in Your Mercy. Dress my soul in Your Strength and Presence.
Lord, You have always supported me and helped me with Your Kindness, You have always empowered me with Your Spirit.

Will You hear me again and give me an answer, so that others may know that You are my God and You have sent me to do Your Will.

Amen.

The Wellspring of Good

Lord, I am ready right now to fulfill Your Will that moves everything living the world. If I have found a blessing before You, may I feel Your Joy in the name of Your Love, Wisdom and Truth.

Lord, place me in the Fire of Your Love!

Lord, what should I do for the triumph of Your Kingdom on Earth and for the Illumination of Your Name before the people.

Lord, teach me to think for my brothers and sisters as You think for them.

Amen.

Prayer of the Mission of the Master

Lord, our God, Eternal Beauty and Light of us all. May the Consonance of Your life embrace our souls.

We direct our souls towards You, the wellspring of all goodness, Who gives life and joy to Your children and comforts them at all times.

Blessed are You, Lord, Who leads us in the Path of Your Light and blesses us through the Spirit of Your boundless Mercy and Limitless Love, through which Your Glory is manifested.

Our hearts have quiet confidence in Your Love that revives us.

We thank You for the beautiful life You have given us, for all good things which You constantly do for us. All goods with which You shower us and surround us come from You.

We thank you for the bright thoughts, lofty feelings and noble impulses which Your Sacred Spirit grants us.

May the Light of Your Wisdom illuminate the minds of all nations. May Your Truth shine in every soul and may Your Love flow through every heart so that the nations may enter into the World of Love and come to know that Life comes from You.

Do that which You have said that all will bow before You and will glorify Your Name.

Support the leaders of the nations, so that they may accept the Principles of the Universal Brotherhood of Light and bring decisions into line with the Divine Plan for Brotherhood and Unity among nations.

May the whole of heaven work with the Master and may His mission be crowned with success. May the Word of the Master enlighten every consciousness, may It be received and applied all over the world.

Awaken the spirit of the Bulgarian nation, of the Slavs and the spirit of all nations which You have called to fulfill their mission.

Support all Your workers, give them strength, knowledge, love and inspiration to work with joy for Your Great Plan. Send even more workers into Your field.

Extend Your Blessing upon us, who cannot do anything without Your power and goodness.

We want to live according to the Law of Love, so as to be able through It to resolve the issues which stand before the door of our souls and to walk in Your Sacred Path.

Send us each day Your peace and Your Joy. Stretch forth Your hand upon us. You have always supported us with Your Love and we will serve You with our whole mind, with our whole heart, with our whole soul and with our whole strength. From You we have learnt the Great Example of Life.

May our life bear abundant fruit for the Work of the Lord Jesus Christ and may it be a holy, living sacrifice, pleasing to Him.

May the Holy Spirit of Christ come into us so as to raise us and to act through us.

Make us a chosen vessel of Your Plan, make us robust, support us to work for the coming of Your Kingdom and its Justice on Earth. Teach us to fulfill constantly Your Kind Will and to glorify Your Name with our life. For the sake of Your Love do all this.

Amen.

Prayer

When praying pray for your love of God. When you pray, stand before God like a child and say:

Lord, bless me! Thank You for everything that You have given me!. Help me to increase the freedom of my soul, the strength of my spirit, the light in my mind, and the goodness of my heart.

Amen.

(From the lecture "Essential Connections", 1937.)

Short Prayers

Prayer

In the self education prayer takes great part. If one wants to influence himself he must turn to God with the following short prayer:

Lord, bless my tongue, so that from it come out sweet, strong and beautiful words.

The sweet words are related to life, the strong- to the human mind, but the beautiful to the human spirit and soul. The sweet, strong, and beautiful words represent material through which man is building the great and the powerful in his life.

(From the lecture "Inner Enlightenment", given on July 15, 1938 5:00 am, Rila mountain.)

Prayer

Teach me, Lord, to serve you thus, as You want me to serve You.

Prayer

Most kindly Lord, pour the Light of Divine Wisdom into my mind, so that I may understand Your Laws; immerse my heart in the Warmth of Your Love, so that I may accomplish the smallest good deed and illuminate my path towards You with the Radiance of Divine Truth, so that I may return to Your Bosom and fulfill Your Will.
Amen.

Prayer

Thank You, Lord, for the great blessing, which You gave us.
We know You as
All-Merciful,
All-Wise,
All-Loving and
All-Kind.
Amen.

Prayer

May Your Light enlighten our minds. With This Light may we solve that Divine question which sits before the door of our souls.
Amen.

Prayer

Bless me, God!

I thank You for all that You have given me.

Help me that the freedom of my soul and the strength of my spirit, the light of my mind and the purity of my heart may be increased.

Lord, I desire that Your Love, Your Wisdom, Your Righteousness and Your Goodness abide within me forever.

May the Kingdom of God be established within us and among us.

May God remove all obstacles before us from the Path to His Kingdom.

God, illuminate our minds and give us light and knowledge so that we may understand Your Will and do It.

Amen.

Prayer

Lord, I wish, with the power of Your Love, to grow within me the Virtues which You have put in my soul from the beginning; I will apply all of my strength on Your vineyard for the fulfillment of Your Will.
Amen.

Prayer

May the Great Spirit of God abide upon my spirit, soul, heart, mind and will. May He embrace them in His bosom and fill them out with the good fruits of His Spirit. May we fulfill the Good and Holy Will of the Father of lights now and always throughout all ages of the future.
Amen.

Prayer

Lord, You are always Kind, You have never left me and You will rescue me now too. I believe in You and to You I leave my weakness.
Amen.
(The Master has said: "With this prayer God always helps".)

Prayer

I am human, a servant of good.
I am a particle of the Great Divine Consciousness.
I am firm like the diamond and bright like the Sun.
I am growing and will grow so I can see the Face of God.
Amen.

Prayer

Lord, purity in the heart, purity in the mind, and purity in the soul I entreat.
Lord, light in the heart, light in the mind, and light in the soul I entreat.
Lord, give strength to my spirit, so I can serve You throughout all my life in Spirit and Truth.
Amen.

Reason, analyze over the powers, which have made these words: "Spirit and Truth"- they are the keys.
The Master

Prayer

Lord, You can do all things! Your Spirit, Whom You have sent to guide me, through You can do all things, and I through Your Spirit can do all things. Help me now in the work that I am starting to

finish it well. Let it be for Your Glory and for the good of my soul.
Amen.

Prayer

Lord, I entreat You, send me an angel to teach me how to do the smallest good, to teach me how to make the smallest act of Love, to teach me the smallest knowledge, to teach me how to give people the smallest freedom, and how to show the smallest mercy.
Amen.

Prayer

May the Lord be glorified as He has written in His book. And after the Lord is glorified as He has written in His book, may His Love be manifested towards my soul and the souls of all of my brothers and sisters.

Amen.

Prayer

Lord, I already live in You. You have given me this mind that I have. You have given me this strength that I have. You have given me the life. In the name of everything which You have given me, I want to serve You.

Lord, what do you want from me? I will fulfill everything that is your will!

Amen.

Prayer

May God of all fullness fill us with His Kind Spirit. Let us fulfill His Kind Will! All-Kind Father of all fullness, in the Name of Your Love, illuminate us with Your Kind

Spirit and fill out our hearts with Your peace.
Amen.

Prayer

Lord, bless me. Thank you for everything, which You have given me. Help my freedom, the strength of my spirit, the light of my mind, and may the goodness of my heart be increased.
Amen.

Prayer

When a spiritual man wants to change anyone of his conditions, it is enough to turn to the Lord with the words:
"Lord, just say a speech. Just say a speech, Lord, our minds to heal. Just say a speech, Lord, our minds to enlighten,

our hearts to heal, and Your Love to incarnate in us, to do Your Will.

Just say a speech."

Prayer

Lord, we want to receive the Spirit of Love.
(3 times)
Lord, we want to receive the Spirit of Wisdom.
(3 times)
Lord we want to receive the Spirit of Truth.
(3 times)
Lord, may Your Name be blessed now and always.
Amen.

(Another variation I found is reading each sentence of the prayer only once.)

Prayer

May God live in us and we live in God. And let Love be a strong connection between us. Not only between us, but between all on Earth. And not only between all on Earth, but also between all in Heaven. And all who live on Earth and Heaven be one.

Amen, so be it!

Prayer

I want to fulfill God's Will, so I can be healthy and useful to myself. I want to find the Kingdom of God and His Justice, so I can be useful to my neighbors. I want to illuminate the Name of God on Earth so that I get connected with all good, reasonable and uplifted souls around the whole world.

Amen.

Prayer

Lord, Your Will be done!
I will accept with joy in my heart all that comes from Your hand, and I will fulfill Your Will without any breakings of Your law.
Amen.

Prayer

Lord, my God, make me to see Your Face. Gladden me for the sake of Your Name. Bless me for the sake of Your mercy. Illuminate me for the sake of your Spirit. Uplift me for the sake of Your Word. Help me for the sake of Your promise. Lead for the sake of Your Truth. Support me for the sake of Your Justice.

And be always blessed, because You are kind, truthful to all.
Amen.

The Lovely Prayer of the Mother:

Lord, bless my child. Guard him/her from all ills and help him/her to develop all the gifts and capabilities, which You have laid in his/her soul.

Motto-Prayer

Lord, I entreat You, strengthen my strivings to direct my personal life in harmony with the Divine.

To live with the consciousness to only serve and study from any given situation in life.

To check and control every act in my personal life, and to evaluate whether I act correctly; whether I am straitening out at any moment my thoughts, feelings, and actions, whether I am feeding myself according to the rules., whether I keep my body in absolute purity, whether I breath deeply, whether I sing.

Instruction:
"For a week choose a prayer and repeat it many times during the day. Take a note how many times you have said it. This experiment will serve you as a topic, which will connect you with the Invisible world."
The Master

FORMULAS

The formulas are uplifting spiritual thoughts given by the Master Beinsa Duno/Peter Dunov for strengthening the spirit, the faith, the mind and health and to help one perfect himself. Some of them are connected with texts from the Bible and the Scriptures.

These formulas are powerful spiritual thoughts if used correctly with full faith and absolutely no doubt in the powers of God they will bring in the desired results.

Many of these formulas are repeated 3 times, as indicated: once for the Divine world, once for the spiritual world and once for the physical world. In my opinion, for maximum benefit it is essential that you think and reason upon them.

Formulas for Protection

Guard yourself from visitation of certain spirits. Those are foes from centuries past. Do not allow them to influence you through the people, so that you are not being attacked from the invisible world.
The Master

Surround yourself: "With Light and peace, with Truth and Purity!" With bright thoughts and formulas, do not pay them any attention and when they feel ignored, they will leave in peace. These are all tests.   *The Master*

In the fulfillment of the Will of God is the strength of the human soul.
(3 times)

"This is one of the most powerful formulas"- has said the Master.

No power in the world is in the condition to stop my Divine growth.

In the Divine plan is for me to grow in virtue.

In the Divine plan is for me to mature in Divine Justice.

In the Divine plan is for me to live in Divine Truth.

In the Divine plan is for me to blossom in Divine Wisdom.

In the Divine plan is for me to ripen in Divine Love.

Therefore I am on the Path of Truth and Life. This right no one can take away form me.

Where God is, there am I also.

(If you say that, you are fencing yourself with a powerful aura and all Bright Brothers are on your side.)

In the name of the Divine Love,
in the name of the Divine Wisdom,
in the name of the Divine Truth,
in which I live and move and have my being,
and with the power of the living Word of
God, may all evil and cunning thoughts be dispersed.

(3 times)

***

Guarding yourself in the morning and evening

Lord of Love, God of Light, disperse all impurities around me.

***

Guard us, Lord, with Your Sacred Name through all the days of our life. We commend our spirit into Your Hands. Guide us with the Light of Your Teaching.

***

I know only One Spirit of Truth and I call upon the Power of that Spirit to surround me off, to protect me.

God of Love, God of Light, Disperse all impure influences around me.

Lord, surround me with your white light. The Spirit of God, the beloved of my soul will do everything for me.
(3 times)

Lord, send your Divine powers to disperse all evil plots around me.

Without Love there is no success.

***

The task of every man is to show his love, to work in this direction, so he can come to the highest level of Love.

***

In the name of God's Love, In the name of God's Wisdom, and in the name of God's Truth, in Which we live and move, and in the name of His Word, let every evil and cunning thought be dispersed.

(For greater effect lift your hands up and at the end you can blow the air out your mouth with something like a whoo sound. You can use this formula against anyone. Look up and do the exercise. The exercise can be made in your thought mentally, but when done with hands it acts stronger, the mind and the heart take part at the same time.)

***

In the name of God's Love, In the name of God's Wisdom and with the power of His Word may all devilish things disappear.
(Whoo sound- blowing air out.)

***

Love, Wisdom, and Truth are Divine Powers with which one can do everything in the world.

***

Fir-Fure-Fen, Tau-be Aumen. (Without fear and darkness in the Boundless Love.)

***

Light, Light, Light. Love, Love, Love. Justice, Justice, Justice.

In need repeat this formula to surround yourself with light and positive powers.

The Master

✼✼✼

When facing certain difficulties and sufferings say this formula: **"Love is coming."**

From these words the evil spirits run away. If you are broke (poor), if you are sick, if you are in disposition say: "Love is coming". Love is a great power from which the bad spirits, the difficulties and the sufferings run away. There is nothing more beautiful for a man to realize, that Love is already coming in the world. In Love is understood the presence of God.

The Master

***

We have the right in this world to grow and mature. This is a Divine process defined by God. No one has the right to stop this Divine process in us. No power in the world has the right to hinder our development. In the Divine plan is for me to develop. Consequently, I am on the road of Truth and Divine life. This right no one can take away from me. It is my own personal right. Where God is, there am I too.

Say this and have no hesitation or fear. When you say this you are already surrounded with the powerful forces of the Bright brothers and God will be on your side, because His Law is for you to grow.
The Master

***

When we want somebody to help and not do any evil to us we focus our eyes between his eyebrows and say in our mind.

God, Who lives in you will do no evil to me.
(3 times)

***

Protect me, Lord with your Kind Spirit. I believe in the One God of Love. I believe in One Teacher of Wisdom. I believe in One Spirit of Truth, upon Whom I call to surround me.

***

Surround me, Lord, with Your Divine Love, with Your Divine light and remove all lower beings, who want to stumble me.

Give them peace and light, and send them to work.

***

Even if you meet a bandit, do not be afraid, but say:

"Lord, I know You in the good and in the bad man. You, Who rule the Universe, won't allow this man to kill me. You will show Your mercy through him."

When the bandit hears these words he will awaken and will give up his intention to kill.

***

When leaving your home say:

"Lord, protect me from great misfortune, sudden death and from evil

enemies. Guard and protect me, Lord and lead everything into Your glory."
The Master

***

Morning Formulas

When you wakeup first stop at the thought what God wants from you today. Before you wash, do a good deed:

a) Call up the best feeling and tell yourself the first word of Love.

b) Call up the most beautiful thought in you mind, and show the nicest light.

c) Then pronounce the holy formula, for the saying of which you must be very positive and have child like spirit:

"Merciful, Holy, and Kind Lord, manifest me the Light of Your Face to do Your Will."
The Master

Lord, help me throughout today's day my behavior to be like that of an angel, my thought to be like the behavior of the Sun, my feelings to be like the behavior of a well spring.

Only the mind brings my happiness. Only the mind brings my strength. Only the mind brings all opportunities from which I can benefit.

I want to do something for God.

***

Long ago, when I was at your age, when I was studying this science, when I was getting up in the morning, I was starting like this:

"Thank you, God, for everything that You have given me and taught me."

And you should start like that. This is a great teaching. If you don't start like this, you will be in eternal darkness, in eternal darkness around yourself. If you apply it the Lord and the angels will smile at you and will help you to become sons of God.
The Master

In order for things to go well, put your hands on top of your head and say:

"Lord, I want to serve you with all of my heart, with all of my mind, with all of my soul and with all of my spirit."
The Master

***

I am a good and reasonable man, because God has created me.

***

I have come on Earth to acquire Love, Wisdom, Truth, Justice, and Virtue. I am an angel-messenger, a servant of God. This is my task, for which I have come on Earth.

***

I have come to bring the good, Love, Wisdom, Truth, Justice. I have come to accept the good, the Love, Wisdom, Truth, and Justice.

***

Lord, look at my hand and tell me what I should do for today. If I have any defect, tell me what it is, and give me a method to straighten it out.

In the morning, at getting up, make an experiment, tell yourself:

"Thank you, Lord, for the great bliss, that you have for us. We know You, that You are All-Merciful, All-Truthful, and All-Wise."

Repeat this continuously for a month and then come to tell me what is the temperature of your soul. This is the whole secret. If you repeat it for 10 months, you will be even better.
The Master

Every morning after you get up, say:

Lord, thank You that I have remained alive so that I can serve You and this day.

And so, when you get up in the morning, do not think that you are a man, woman or a child, but tell yourself:

"I am an angel-messenger, a servant of God. This is my task for which I have come down on Earth."

I want to become a learned man.

This thought goes to the mind and begins to feed the cells. If you do that the whole year, at the end of the year you will have a small result. Your mind will get cleared, and you will grasp things correctly.

***

Today I want to do more than yesterday.

***

Bless, my soul the Lord, for all goodness which He gave me.

***

I believe in the God within me, I believe in the God outside of me.
(3 times)

***

Lord, help me to do the work, that is in store for me for today in such a way as You understand it.

***

May God be glorified as He has written in His book. And after He is glorified as He has written in His holy book, may His Love be manifested in my soul and the souls of all my brothers and sisters.

(This formula is to be pronounced only in the morning.)

***

When you wake up and get up in the morning, do not rush to wash, but meditated for 5-10 min., turn to God and to the lofty beings, and say:

"Lord, I have little knowledge, enlighten my mind, to accept and fulfill Your Will. Give me a method to realize Your wishes, which You have defined."

If you say this, there won't pass a long time and you will receive an answer to your prayer, you will feel in your soul quietness- a joy. As you act like that, you will have harmony within yourself.

✳✳✳

Task for one year:
Every morning and evening to be pronounced at 8 o clock:

"I will live in Love, as Christ has written, that life will be set right with Love. Whatever the Lord has written, I will live according to His Law. May life be rectified as He has said."

✳✳✳

Task for a year: To be said in the morning, noon, and evening:

"The Lord lives in me, I am good."

***

Every morning put a ring with a precious stone on every finger and say:

"I want to give movement to the Divine within me, to be noble, just, musical, with striving to beauty and to have a good attitude to people."

***

Every morning pronounce this formula:

"If you love Me, you will keep my word."

If you love Christ you will keep His Word. It bares in itself great Wisdom, which uplifts and strengthens a man's will and makes people free, happy and blessed. When you pronounce this verse, the string with which you are attached to something or somebody will fall and light

will come in your mind.
Misunderstandings, quarrels, everything that you have between yourselves, tear them with this verse.
The Master

✽✽✽

Lord, I thank You that I have risen, I thank You that I am alive.
Tell me what I can do for You today.

✽✽✽

Lord, give me Strength, Life and Health to work for Your Great Plan.

✽✽✽

(With lifted up hands)
Lord, I ask You to pour living cosmic forces into me, which penetrate each cell of my body, to bring vitality and health into it, to strengthen my spirit, so that I

can fulfill the task for which I have come to Earth.

Go out each morning and turn your back first to the south, then to the north, and after a little while to the East, and stand like that for one hour from seven to eight. Direct your mind upward and say:

LORD, I WANT TO TRY YOU! YOU ALONE ARE THE CREATOR OF ALL THINGS! THERE IS NONE OTHER IN THE WORLD THAT SAVES, BUT YOU!

Lord, enlighten my mind. Give health to everyone who needs it and to me as well.

***

When seeing the Sunrise we must consciously connect with it, so that its powers can flow through our organism. The formula is pronounced also when we expose our backs to the Sunrays.

Lord, thank You for the sacred energy of Divine life which You are sending us with the Sun's rays.
I feel livingly how it penetrates into all my organs bringing strength, life and health to my whole body. It is the expression of Your Love towards us.
Thank You!

***

If things get messed up, go see the Sunrise. When you inhale say:

"My things will be set alright."

When the light dawns on you.

"My things will be set alright. Everything in Nature says that my things will be set alright."

Love dawned on me, expanded my soul, strengthened my spirit and kindness incarnated in me. I will become bright and clear like the Sun.

Every day at sunrise have a wish to have Love in your heart and Truth in your mind. Thus during the whole day you will be joyful and merry. If you go out at sunrise, realize deep in yourself, that you will know God today more than you have known Him up to now. If at sunrise you realize that, you accept more of God's Love and the Divine life, then the Sun's light will have healing effect.

Formulas for Deep Breathing

✶✶✶

For the absorption of vital energy – prana do deep breathing. If you want to be patient, you have to learn to hold your air for a longer time. Your patience depend on how long you can hold the air in your lungs. There are adepts who can hold the air for 4 hours. There is prana that you receive through the left nostril and another through the right. Through the left nostril one receives the magnetic current, which has connection with the Solar plexus and is called "Sun current". Through the right nostril is accepted the electrical current, *which has connection with the* main brain *and is called "lunar current". The first has connection with the heart, but the second with the mind. When we want to develop the mind more, we accept the air from the right nostril and release it through the left. We do that so we can establish balance between the mind and the heart, and also to establish the balance between the electricity and the magnetism. When we switch the nostril and breath once from one and then from the other we balance both currents.*

1. Do 20 inhales and exhales and say: "Lord, I believe in You!"

Uplift your subjective mind higher than the
   objective.
2. Say in your mind:

When inhaling: "Lord, thank You, that You have entered in me."

When holding your breath: "Lord, thank you that You are in me."

When exhaling: "Lord, thank You, that You left Your blessing in me."

3. Say in your mind:

When inhaling: "Lord, thank you, that you have put in the air Your blessing which I accept together with the air."

When exhaling: "Thank You, Lord, that You left Your blessing in me."

4. Say in your mind:

When inhaling: "May the Name of God be glorified within me."

When Holding your breath: "May the Kingdom of God and His Justice dwell within me."

When exhaling: "May the Will of God be done."

These breathing exercises are done first through the left, then through the right nostril.
If these formulas are pronounced regularly- in the morning, at noon, and evening, but also at any other time, one can realize 75% of his plans in life.

5. Say in your mind:

When inhaling: "Thank You very much, Lord, for the goods which You have given me."

When holding your breath: "Thank You very much, Lord, for the goods which You have given me."

When exhaling: "Thank You very much, Lord, for the goods which You have given me."

6. Say in your mind:

When inhaling: Thank You, Lord, for the Divine Life which You have put in the air and which I receive together with it.

When holding your breath: This Divine Life permeates my whole body and brings in strength, life and health everywhere.

When exhaling: This Divine life strengthens me and I manifest it outwardly through my actions.

7. I want my heart to beat rhythmically, to merge with the pulse of the Sun and to correctly send its energies throughout my whole organism, like the Sun sending its energies throughout the whole world.

8. You can chose some nice sentences from the Bible for the same purpose or verse from the Gospel of John, upon which you can reason during the breathing. Or you can say the "Lord's Prayer" in your mind when inhaling, same thing when holding your breath, and exhaling one time on each. These breathing exercises you can do in the morning, at noon, and in the evening ten times. You can also say "The Good Prayer" during your inhaling, holding your breath, and exhaling. Or you can say three times "strength, life, health" during each inhaling, holding of your breath, and exhaling. You can do this exercise in the morning, at noon, and in the evening ten times.

9. *Inhale through the left nostril and say in your mind:*

"Only God's Love is Love".

Say the same formula when holding your breath, and when exhaling through the right nostril as well. (You can switch the inhaling and exhaling nostril sides after each exercise.) This exercise is done in the morning, noon, and evening ten times each time.

10. *Say in your mind:*

Inhaling through the left nostril. "May the Name of God be glorified within me".

When holding your breath: "May the Kingdom of God and God's Justice be established in me".

When exhaling through the right nostril: "May the Will of God be done".

(8, 9, and 10 breathing exercises are from a letter of brother Boyan Boev to some young disciples of the Master written on 12.19.1952. Switching of the nostrils when inhaling and exhaling is my suggestion. I have read in some lectures about the switching and have tried it myself and I received better results.)

***

Formula Before Meal

Lord, thank You for the abundance which You have given us. Let it reach all people on the face of the Earth. Let all have what we have to eat.

***

Formulas for Healing

I am ready to serve God.
I am serving God.
I work for God.
So I must be healthy, and I am healthy.

※※※

When you are with somebody who is sick or suffering hold his hand and say in your mind:

Lord, You are Powerful and Mighty. If You wish, You can free this man from his sufferings.

※※※

If you are sick say:

"I love You, Lord!"

and you will be healed. God's power is manifested in the difficult moments in life.

He, who's consciousness is awakened can heal himself only with his thought. When he gets sick he right away uplifts himself in his thought and there he rectifies his mistake, which was the cause for his illness. Then, he gets down to heart, where he also rectifies his mistake, which has caused the illness. And at last, he enters the area of his will where he rectifies his mistake too. Then he says:

"Let it be the Will of God".

When he says that, his illness and difficulty disappear.

Love is a mighty power, which cures all diseases. If you pronounce the word "Love" correctly, you can cure yourself. for example if you have rheumatism in your leg, say deeply in you with faith and trust in the Great:

"God is Love and in Love diseases do not exist."

If you say these words 2-3 times, your disease will disappear. If you say the words: "God is Love", get up off your bed right away.

✳✳✳

Love is coming.
(3 times)

✳✳✳

Thank You, Lord for sending me this suffering. Thank You, Lord, for sending me this joy. Lord, thank You for everything that you are sending me. Everything is from God. This is the Will of God.

✳✳✳

Lord in You I trust, on You I give my burden. I love You, Lord. Thank You, Lord that you have decided to cleanse me.

✳✳✳

When in sleeplessness say:

"This night I will sleep. I must sleep and I will beg from the Limitless Consciousness help so it can send me sleep."

(t is pronounced in the morning so it can act during the day)

When in sleeplessness say:

"Lord, I am powerless, You are mighty- manifest Yourself."

When you have pain somewhere, put your hands on top of the place where the pain is located and say the following.

And this is Eternal Life to know You, the One, the Only True God and Jesus Christ Whom You have sent. This is eternal life to know Love.

Put your palms upon the sick place and say:

I live in God and God lives in me. In God does not exist any illness. Therefore I must be healthy and I am healthy.

If your faith in God is strong, there won't pass half an hour and your pain will disappear.

The Lord is kind.

The master says, that with these words all diseases are healed.

I am mobilized to serve God.

When we say these words to the illness, it goes away.

Lord, You are always kind. You have never left me, and now You will rescue me. I believe in You, and to You I leave my weakness.

***

Lord, in You is all of my trust. Help me, send me Your help. I promise to serve You and to dedicated my life to You.

***

Lord, from now on I will dedicate all of my life to You, I will work for You. Leave me on Earth.

***

I, who serve the Lord, want my body to be healthy, because I belong to the Lord. It is a cell of the Great Cosmos, and that is why it must be healthy.

I will give you a way to diagnose and to know whether you love God. You are coughing a lot. Say:

"I love the Lord!"

If you coughing stops, you truly love God. If it does not stop, you don't love Him.

You are poor. Say:

"I love God!"

If your poverty leaves you, you love God. If it does not, you do not love Him.

※※※

You are in discomfort, say:

"I believe in God outside of me, I believe in God within me."
"Me and my Father are one." Thus has said Christ.

***

God is Love, God is Light, God is Life, may His name be glorified now and always throughout all His times.

***

Put your left hand on the left side of your head and say with confidence:

Lord, for Your glory, pour a chrism of health and life into my cells, for I can serve You with joy and merriment.

***

Purity, purity pour, Lord, into my body, my soul, and my spirit!

***

When you feel in discomfort, sour, nervous, say the following:

Lord, warm up my heart with Your Love!

***

When Your mind is darkened say:

Lord, enlighten my mind with Your Spirit.

Or:

Lord, give light to my mind through Your Spirit.

***

I am mobilized, I have work to do. I am serving God and therefore all spirits who cause diseases must go away.

***

When you are unwell, say:

God is now fine. All world, all angels are joyful. Then why should I stumble myself?

If you are sick say:

Lord, from now on I will serve You with all of my mind, with all of my heart, with all of my soul, and with all of my strength.

Today people die prematurely, because they do not work consciously. They don't know how to work and for who, so they can prolong their lives. If they sincerely wish to serve God, to do His Will, their lives will be prolonged. Man must not leave for the other world before finishing his work on Earth.

I will prolong my life.

With these words we can prolong our lives.

***

Make an experiment with yourself or others when on death bed, say:

Lord, from now on I will dedicate all my life for You! I will work for You! Leave me on Earth!

And make a confession before God in your soul.

***

Somebody gets sick to death, let him turn to God with the words:

Lord, if this, which is preached to us in Your Name is true, help me to get healthy! I promise that I will serve You!

Whoever makes the experiment sincerely, pure heartedly, will come to the conviction himself, that the Lord is alive! I want you to know This Lord and be convinced in my words.

***

When you feel a burden in your stomach, stand up, put your hands on your stomach, with the right hand on top of the left, with the thumbs against each other and say:

All of my things are set right!

***

Whatever disease you have, hold the sick place and say:

I will serve the Lord!

Enjoy everything, because it was determined to happen.

***

Make an experiment with the words: "God is Love", to see what a power is hidden in them. Put these words in your mind, in your heart and in your will, and you will see if you are sick you will get healed. If until now you were looking, from now on you will see, if you were only feeling, from now on you will love. Great, and mighty is the power of Love, but you have to know how to apply it.

***

I will be set right in my thoughts, feelings and deeds, so I can see life and serve consciously.

Analyze every word and think about its structure and meaning. Somebody says: "I don't have money!" Riches, happiness, joy lie in the inner understanding of life.

***

Raise your right hand up and say:

Lord, I call upon all reasonable forces, which fill the whole Cosmos with their building powers, which build and heal, I wish to connect with them **so they** remove all impure powers, which are obstacles for my health.

***

The Great Spirit of the Universe, Who revives all cells, may He gift me life and health.

***

God is Love.
God is Light.
God is Life.

In these words is hidden great power, when pronounced they serve to heal the sick.

In the man's body there are specific cells- doctors, they are better than the best doctors on Earth. They stay in man and say: "Master, just give us your opinions and orders, whatever you want we will do it." They can heal us excellently. Ask them and say:

Please, collect all data necessary for my healing and create all conditions for work.

Say it with faith, without doubt and with good disposition, otherwise the law won't work.

***

Say to the disease:

God, Whom I serve is commanding you to untie me. I am going to do His work, and I must surely do it.

***

An English woman was sick for 12 years- she almost became handicapped. One day she came across a book "Healing by Divine means", where it was said, that when you come to believe in God and accept His Love, one can heal any disease, and she devoted her life in service to God. She told herself calmly, but firmly:

" I accept God's Love for a foundation of my life".
She kept repeating these words for a long time, persistently and like a miracle she got off the bed. Thus are being healed

those who patiently wait for their healing. They were inwardly prepared. Christ has told them: "Let it be according to your faith". *Such was the case with the woman who had bleeding for 12 year, and with the man who was sick for 38 years, with the son of that mother, who Christ resurrected (Luke 7:13-15).*

Commandment of the Master

Love the perfect path of Truth and Life. Place Good as the foundation of your house, Justice as a measure, Love as an adornment, Wisdom as a wall of defense, Truth as the light. Only then will you come to know Me and I will reveal Myself to you.

The disciple must have:

A heart as pure as crystal,
A mind as bright as the Sun,
A soul as vast as the universe,
A spirit as mighty as God and one with God.
(3 times)

God reigns in Heaven,
God reigns on Earth,
blessed be His Name.
(3 times)

Lord, our God, may Your Kingdom come on Earth, as it is in Heaven, and may all nations which You have called take their place in Your Kingdom, so they can serve You with joy and gladness.
(3 times)

May the Peace of God and the Blessing of God encompass and enfold the whole Earth.
(3 times)

I have to be in agreement with the great conscious Love, with the Divine Spirit, and I will act as reasonably as He acts.

God's Love brings fullness of life,
God's Wisdom brings fullness of light,
God's Truth brings perfect freedom!

***

Great is God in His Love!
Great is God in His Wisdom!

Great is God in His Truth!
In His Love God teaches,
In His Wisdom God enlightens,
In His Truth God liberates.
Merciful and compassionate is the Lord
And His Kindness is above all things.
His gladness supports everything.
Everything lives and moves in the Lord.
He is gladness and joy in all that lives
in the world.

Lord, we wish to receive the Spirit of Love.
(3 times)
Lord, we wish to receive the Spirit of Wisdom. *(3 times)*
Lord, we wish to receive the Spirit of Truth.
(3 times)
Blessed is Your Name, Lord, now and forever.

***

Lord, may Your Spirit of Love, Your Spirit of Wisdom, Your Spirit of Truth arise in our hearts.

May we be
As pure as Light,
As transparent as water,
As abundant as Love,
As radiant as Truth,
As harmonious as Wisdom,
As firm and unshakeable as Justice,
As stable as Virtue.

God is Love.
God is All-wise.
God is All-kind.

***

Great are You, Lord.
Great are Your Deeds.
Great is Your Name above all.
I send my love to You.
In everything and everyone
I see You and I love You.
I will serve You throughout the whole eternity.

***

Greeting

When meeting somebody say:

– There is no Love like God's Love!

Reply:

– Only God's Love is Love!

***

The Sacred Formula

Merciful, Holy and Kind Lord, show me the
Light of Your Face, so that I may do Your
Will.

For Your sake, Lord, Who has been living in my soul from all Eternity, I will study and serve You.

Lord, I wish with my whole heart, with my whole mind, with my whole soul and strength to fulfill Your Good Will, without any exception.

Trust in the Lord with all your heart, and do not lean on your own reasoning. In all your ways know Him, and He will make your paths straight.

May Love, Faith and Hope unite in our hearts, and may God be glorified in our souls.
(3 times)

I will serve God with all my mind, with all my heart and all my will.
I will walk in the Lord's Path with my love, my faith and my strength.
And I will come to know God in my life with my heart and my mind.
Amen.

The Eternal Life exists that I may come to know You, the One True God and Jesus Christ Whom You have sent.

God is Love.

"If you love Me, you will keep My Word."

Thank You, Lord, for giving me life and health. Fill my heart with love and strengthen my will so that I may fulfill Your Will. May everything I do be done in Your Name and for Your Glory.

Amen.

***

Lord, I ask You to fill me with the energies of Life. May they penetrate every cell of my body, bringing it strength and

health; may they strengthen my spirit in fulfilling the task assigned to me on Earth.
Amen.

***

God has placed everything in my soul. I wish to do the Will of God, to fulfill the Divine Plan, whatever God has intended for me. May the Will of God be done. I will work as God has ordained.

***

Lord, may the Divine which You have deposited in my soul before the creation of the world, grow within me.

***

God is Spirit and whoever serves Him must serve Him in Spirit and in Truth!

***

God is Love and those who know Him, must serve Him in Spirit and in Truth!

***

Christ says:

"As God loves me, so I love you."

And you must say:

"As God loves Christ, and as Christ loves us, so we must love our neighbors."

***

When having difficulties say:

No matter how difficult this work is, I will finish it with God and the Spirit, Who leads me.

***

When nervous and you feel you don't have patience with something, put Love in your soul and say: "With Love I can endure anything!" Some foolish thought comes in your mind, do not deny it, but tell yourself: "With Wisdom I can do anything!" A lie comes, don't deny it, but tell yourself: "With Truth I can do anything!" Then you draw strength. And so when it comes to apply the spiritual laws, always use positive words and phrases.

***

Lord, may everything be for Your Glory and for the Good of my soul.
(to be said after a prayer)

***

May we be ready to receive the Word of God in our minds, in our hearts and in our souls and then to apply it.
Amen, so be it.
(3 times)

***

In time of desperation say:

Lord, I bless You thousands and millions of times.
(3 times)

(This formula is very important; it has a magical strength. When things get really bad, pronounce it and see what will happen within your soul. Only say this formula when you do not think anything bad. And when you say it, your path will always open up everywhere and it is the most natural means to deal with your

difficulties and to achieve everything, for which you were born.)

My heart is warm, my soul is fresh, my mind is bright, my spirit is strong, because I live in the law of Love in which there are no changes.

Lord, may Your Love, Your Wisdom, Your Truth, Your Justice and Your Goodness dwell within me.

The faith in which I live will bring Divine Harmony into the strivings of my heart.

✳︎✳︎✳︎

All-Kindly Father of all fullness, in the Name of Your Love, illuminate me with Your Kind Spirit and fill my heart with Your peace.

✳︎✳︎✳︎

For God so loved the world that He gave His only begotten Son that whoever believes in Him shall not perish but have eternal life.
(John 3:16)

✳︎✳︎✳︎

But, seek first the Kingdom of God and His righteousness and all other things shall be added unto you.
(Matthew 6:33)

✳✳✳

I sanctify the Name of God,
I seek the Kingdom of God and His Righteousness,
I do the Will of God.
(The Master often pronounced this formula in front of the disciples.)

✳✳✳

Lord, Give Peace and Light to each soul.

✳✳✳

May God's Peace abide, and may God's joy and God's gladness dawn in our hearts.
(3 times)
(given in the PanEuRhythmy)

***

Lord, send Your blessing upon this house.
(when you visit a house)

***

Lord, I thank You for visiting me through this person.
(when a guest comes to visit you)

***

God of Love is not the God of the dead, but the God of the living.
I am alive and this God is within me. With Him I can do everything. Our will is stronger than any difficulty.

***

May my thoughts be as radiant as the Sun.

May my feelings be as pure as water from mountain springs!

***

Without fear, without darkness, forward into the boundless Love!

***

Without fear into the boundless Love!

***

Without fear, without darkness, in peace and in light.

***

Only the bright path of Wisdom leads to Truth.
Life is hidden it the Truth.
Life is founded on Truth.

Always be faithful, true, pure and kind, and the Lord of Peace will fill your heart with all goodness.

Man must be faithful in Love,
truthful in Wisdom,
pure in Truth and
kind in applying Justice.
(3 times)

Formulas When in Difficulty

When in difficulties you may say to your soul:
God is with you, you will prevail, your victory is my victory.

I believe only in One God of Wisdom and in One Spirit of Truth.

The Priceless Formula

However difficult this work is, I will finish it with God and with the Spirit Who guides me.
(when in great difficulties)

Lord, all things are possible for You. Your Spirit, Who You have sent to guide us can do everything through You. And we can do everything through Your Spirit.
Amen.

Everything is possible for God.

I live in God and with His Wisdom I can achieve everything.
(when you encounter a contradiction)

This will be arranged, this will be arranged, this will be arranged in a way we do not know.
(3 times)

Lord of Forces, send The Holy Spirit of Power and illuminate my room in Your Light and with the Strength of Your Spirit, surround my bed with the fire circle of Your Love, so that my room and my house are protected of evil influences.

※※※

If evil comes to you, do not attack it, but only defend yourself. If a temptation comes on you, quietly say this to yourself.

God is Love, God is Wisdom,
I am Goodness, I am Truth.
(3 times)

This formula is a powerful weapon against evil. Make way for God within yourself and manifest His Love and Wisdom.

※※※

May Love, Wisdom, and Truth begin to reign in our souls. Thus we open our hearts for the Lord, Who is now among us. May His name be glorified.   (3 times)
May this thought remain in you throughout all conditions of your life, without having any fear.

***

Lord, may Your Peace and Your Joy be with us always so that our hearts and minds can be illuminated and we may serve You with our whole heart, with our whole mind, with our whole soul and with our whole strength.

***

Lord, I ask You to send me an angel to teach me the smallest knowledge, to teach me how to do the smallest good and to show the smallest act of love, how to give people the smallest freedom and to manifest the smallest mercy.

***

I WANT YOU TO BE MUSICAL FROM HEAD TO TOE.
(Music is a method for improving life. No matter what field you are in, you

cannot think correctly if you are not musical. Likewise, you will not be able to feel or act correctly if you are not musical.)

***

Love, study, keep silent, endure, forgive, pursue your path and do not forget God!

***

Always be glad! Pray without ceasing! Give thanks for everything. Do not extinguish the Spirit.

***

Place Truth in your soul and you will acquire the freedom, which you seek.

Place Wisdom in your mind – Light will come and knowledge will give you its aid.

Place Purity in your heart – Love will come and the True Life will begin.

***

I should think like God,
I should love as He loves.

***

May the Kingdom of God come on Earth and may I be a bearer of His Light.
(3 times)

***

God is Love which Christ has received.
Christ is Love which we have received.
We are Love which we are now manifesting.
Blessed be the Lord!
(3 times)

***

Christ is the Man of Abundant power,
Christ is the Man of Abundant faith,

Christ is the Man of Abundant love.

I love God and because of Him I love the souls of all people.

And you be perfect, as Your Heavenly Father is perfect.
Perfecting of Love will be the meaning of my life.
Perfect Love casts out every fear and brings peace and gladness to the spirit.

I will lie down in peace and sleep, because only You, Lord, make me live in safety.

***

The disciple inevitably will go through inner struggles and contradictions, but he must not become discouraged, let him say the following formula:

My soul is with you God, You will be victorious!
I know One God of Love, One Teacher of Wisdom and One Spirit of Truth, which we call upon to come with its life-giving power to disperse all evil influences.
(3 times)

Lord, thank You that You have given me an excellent mind in which You placed Your Wisdom, as well as an excellent heart in which You have placed Your Love.
I wish to serve You with this Love and Wisdom.

For the sake of You, Lord, Whom I have carried in my soul from eternity, I will listen to You and serve You.

God is Light.
Angels are Warmth.
People are Kindness.
(3 times)

God is Light within me.
My spirit is Warmth.
I am Kindness.
(3 times)

***

Today reason upon these sentences:

Through Love, Wisdom and Truth everything can be achieved.
Through life, knowledge and freedom everything is achievable.

Apply these things in yourself, so you can be joyful and glad. When you are joyful and glad, the Lord will dwell in you and you will dwell in the Lord.
The road of the Righteous is a road of dawning.

(From the lecture "Values and opportunities". 07/21/1937 5:00 a.m.)

There is no love like God's Love!
Only God's Love is Love!
There is no wisdom like God's Wisdom.
Only God's Wisdom is Wisdom.
There is no Truth like God's Truth.
Only God's Truth is Truth.
There is no Justice like God's Justice.

Only God's Justice is Justice.
There is no virtue like God's Virtue.
Only God's Virtue is Virtue.
There is no power like the Power of the Spirit.
Only the Power of the Spirit is God's Power.
There is no glory like the Glory of Christ.
Only the Glory of Christ is God's Glory.

The abundance of God's Good brings Life.

Love gives birth to Good. Good brings life, light, and freedom to our souls.

***

Slowly raise your hands above your head and with fingers touching each other say:

And this is Eternal Life to know You, the One, the Only True God and Christ Whom You have sent.

Then put your hands close above your head and say:

If my words abide in you and you abide in Me, I and my Father will come to you and will make our dwelling within you, and I will reveal Myself to you.

Lower down your hands towards you pronouncing:

You are, Lord, the Way! I will walk Lord, in Your Way together with You.
(3 times)

With this formula noisy and bad spirits are chased away.
I am mobilized, I have work to do, I serve God.
If you want to serve with me together, stay. If not, leave!

I have in disposition inexhaustible wealth.
I live in the abundance of Divine Love, I breathe the light of Divine Wisdom, I move in the Great Divine Truth, which brings freedom and scope to souls, as I put in movement everything which God gives me.

***

I wish my heart to become rhythmical, to merge with the pulse of the Sun, and to send its energy to the whole organism, just as the Sun sends its energy to the whole world.

***

You, Supreme, Who blesses and creates, set right everything in me and around me.
Come, rectify my mind, may I think right!
Come, rectify my heart, may Living Love well up in it.

***

Evening Formulas
(to be said at bed time)

If you are very weary, or have no time to say a special prayer in the evening, then say:

Lord, be merciful to me.

I will do Your will.

***

Lord, may Your blessing come upon me.
(Spend a few minutes in reasoning.)

***

Lord, thank You for all good things, for all blessings which You are sending me.

***

Lord, surround me with Your Light and protect me during the time of my nightly rest.
I am going up to study, to pray and to work.

***

May God be glorified in the Brotherhood of Light and may the

Brothers of Light be glorified in the Love of God.
   (3 times)

   Which is the most important thing in life?- Prayer.

PSALMS

Psalm 91 *(New International Version)*

1 He who dwells in the shelter of the Most High will rest in the shadow of the Almighty. **2** I will say of the LORD, "He is my refuge and my fortress, my God, in whom I trust." **3** Surely he will save you from the fowler's snare and from the deadly pestilence. **4** He will cover you with his feathers, and under his wings you will find refuge; his faithfulness will be your shield and rampart. **5** You will not fear the terror of night, nor the arrow that flies by day, **6** nor the pestilence that stalks in the darkness, nor the plague that destroys at midday. **7** A thousand may fall at your side, ten thousand at your right hand, but it will not come near you. **8** You will only observe with your eyes and see the punishment of the wicked. **9** If you make the Most High your dwelling-- even the LORD, who is my refuge-- **10** then no harm will befall you, no disaster will come near your tent. **11** For he will command his angels concerning you to guard you in all your ways; **12** they will lift you up in their hands, so that you will not strike your foot against a stone. **13** You will tread upon the lion and the cobra; you will trample the great lion and the serpent. **14** "Because he loves me," says the LORD, "I will rescue him; I will protect him, for he acknowledges my name. **15** He will call upon me, and I will answer him; I will be with him in trouble, I will deliver him and honor him. **16** With long life will I satisfy him and show him my salvation."

Psalm 23 (New International Version)

A psalm of David.
1 The LORD is my shepherd, I shall not be in want. 2 He makes me lie down in green pastures, he leads me beside quiet waters, 3 he restores my soul. He guides me in paths of righteousness for his name's sake. 4 Even though I walk through the valley of the shadow of death, I will fear no evil, for you are with me; your rod and your staff, they comfort me 5 You prepare a table before me in the presence of my enemies. You anoint my head with oil; my cup overflows. 6 Surely goodness and love will follow me all the days of my life, and I will dwell in the house of the LORD forever.

Psalm 133 (New International Version)

A song of ascents. Of David.
1 How good and pleasant it is when brothers live together in unity! 2 It is like precious oil poured on the head, running down on the beard, running down on Aaron's beard, down upon the collar of his robes. 3 It is as if the dew of Hermon were falling on Mount Zion. For there the LORD bestows his blessing, even life forevermore.

Psalm 117 (New International Version)

1 Praise the LORD, all you nations; extol him, all you peoples. 2 For great is his love toward us, and the faithfulness of the LORD endures forever. Praise the LORD.

Psalm 121 (New International Version)

A song of ascents.
1 I lift up my eyes to the hills-- where does my help come from? 2 My help comes from the LORD, the Maker of heaven and earth. 3 He will not let your foot slip-- he who watches over you will not slumber; 4 indeed, he who watches over Israel will neither slumber nor sleep. 5 The LORD watches over you-- the LORD is your shade at your right hand; 6 the sun will not harm you by day, nor the moon by night. 7 The LORD will keep you from all harm-- he will watch over your life; 8 the LORD will watch over your coming and going both now and forevermore.

Psalm 61 (New International Version)

For the director of music. With stringed instruments. Of David.

1 Hear my cry, O God; listen to my prayer. 2 From the ends of the earth I call to you, I call as my heart grows faint; lead me to the rock that is higher than I. 3 For you have been my refuge, a strong tower against the foe. 4 I long to dwell in your tent forever and take refuge in the shelter of your wings. "Selah" 5 For you have heard my vows, O God; you have given me the heritage of those who fear your name. 6 Increase the days of the king's life, his years for many generations. 7 May he be enthroned in God's presence forever; appoint your love and faithfulness to protect him. 8 Then will I ever sing praise to your name and fulfill my vows day after day.

Psalm 143 (New International Version)

A psalm of David.
1 O LORD, hear my prayer, listen to my cry for mercy; in your faithfulness and

righteousness come to my relief. 2 Do not bring your servant into judgment, for no one living is righteous before you. 3The enemy pursues me, he crushes me to the ground; he makes me dwell in darkness like those long dead. 4 So my spirit grows faint within me; my heart within me is dismayed. 5 I remember the days of long ago; I meditate on all your works and consider what your hands have done. 6 I spread out my hands to you; my soul thirsts for you like a parched land. "Selah" 7 Answer me quickly, O LORD; my spirit fails. Do not hide your face from me or I will be like those who go down to the pit. 8Let the morning bring me word of your unfailing love, for I have put my trust in you. Show me the way I should go, for to you I lift up my soul. 9 Rescue me from my enemies, O LORD, for I hide myself in you. 10 Teach me to do your will, for you are my God; may your good Spirit lead me on level ground.11 For your name's sake, O LORD, preserve my life; in your righteousness, bring me out of trouble. 12 In your unfailing love, silence my enemies; destroy all my foes, for I am your servant.

Psalm 27 (New International Version)

Of David.
1 The LORD is my light and my salvation-- whom shall I fear? The LORD is the stronghold of my life-- of whom shall I be afraid? 2 When evil men advance against me to devour my flesh, when my enemies and my foes attack me, they will stumble and fall. 3 Though an army besiege me, my heart will not fear; though war break out against me, even then will I be confident. 4 One thing I ask of the LORD, this is what I seek: that I may dwell in the house of the LORD all the days of my life, to gaze upon the beauty of the LORD and to seek him in his temple. 5 For in the day of trouble he will keep me safe in his dwelling; he will hide me in the shelter

of his tabernacle and set me high upon a rock. 6 Then my head will be exalted above the enemies who surround me; at his tabernacle will I sacrifice with shouts of joy; I will sing and make music to the LORD. 7 Hear my voice when I call, O LORD; be merciful to me and answer me. 8 My heart says of you, "Seek his face!" Your face, LORD, I will seek. 9 Do not hide your face from me, do not turn your servant away in anger; you have been my helper. Do not reject me or forsake me, O God my Savior. 10 Though my father and mother forsake me, the LORD will receive me. 11 Teach me your way, O LORD; lead me in a straight path because of my oppressors. 12 Do not turn me over to the desire of my foes, for false witnesses rise up against me, breathing out violence. 13 I am still confident of this: I will see the goodness of the LORD in the land of the living. 14 Wait for the LORD; be strong and take heart and wait for the LORD.

Psalm 19 (New International Version)

For the director of music. A psalm of David.
1 The heavens declare the glory of God; the skies proclaim the work of his hands. 2 Day after day they pour forth speech; night after night they display knowledge. 3 There is no speech or language where their voice is not heard. 4 Their voice goes out into all the earth, their words to the ends of the world. In the heavens he has pitched a tent for the sun, 5 which is like a bridegroom coming forth from his pavilion, like a champion rejoicing to run his course. 6 It rises at one end of the heavens and makes its circuit to the other; nothing is hidden from its heat. 7 The law of the LORD is perfect, reviving the soul. The statutes of the LORD are trustworthy, making wise the simple. 8 The precepts of the LORD are right, giving joy to the heart. The commands of the LORD are radiant, giving light to the eyes. 9 The fear of the

LORD is pure, enduring forever. The ordinances of the LORD are sure and altogether righteous. 10 They are more precious than gold, than much pure gold; they are sweeter than honey, than honey from the comb. 11 By them is your servant warned; in keeping them there is great reward. 12 Who can discern his errors? Forgive my hidden faults. 13 Keep your servant also from willful sins; may they not rule over me. Then will I be blameless, innocent of great transgression. 14 May the words of my mouth and the meditation of my heart be pleasing in your sight, O LORD, my Rock and my Redeemer.

Psalm 103 (New International Version)
Of David.
1 Praise the LORD, O my soul; all my inmost being, praise his holy name. 2 Praise the LORD, O my soul, and forget not all his benefits-- 3 who forgives all

your sins and heals all your diseases, 4 who redeems your life from the pit and crowns you with love and compassion, 5 who satisfies your desires with good things so that your youth is renewed like the eagle's. 6 The LORD works righteousness and justice for all the oppressed. 7 He made known his ways to Moses, his deeds to the people of Israel: 8 The LORD is compassionate and gracious, slow to anger, abounding in love.9 He will not always accuse, nor will he harbor his anger forever; 10 he does not treat us as our sins deserve or repay us according to our iniquities. 11 For as high as the heavens are above the earth, so great is his love for those who fear him; 12 as far as the east is from the west, so far has he removed our transgressions from us. 13 As a father has compassion on his children, so the LORD has compassion on those who fear him; 14 for he knows how we are formed, he remembers that we are dust. 15 As for man, his days are like grass, he flourishes like a flower of the field; 16 the wind blows over it and it is gone, and its place remembers it no more. 17 But from everlasting to everlasting the LORD's love is with those who fear him, and his righteousness with their children's children-- 18 with those who keep his covenant and remember to obey his precepts. 19 The LORD has established his throne in heaven, and his kingdom rules over all. 20 Praise the LORD, you his angels, you mighty ones who do his bidding, who obey his word. 21 Praise the LORD, all his heavenly hosts, you his servants who do his will. 22 Praise the LORD, all his works everywhere in his dominion. Praise the LORD, O my soul.

Psalm 112 (New International Version)

1 Praise the LORD. Blessed is the man who fears the LORD, who finds great

delight in his commands. 2 His children will be mighty in the land; the generation of the upright will be blessed. 3Wealth and riches are in his house, and his righteousness endures forever. 4 Even in darkness light dawns for the upright, for the gracious and compassionate and righteous man. 5 Good will come to him who is generous and lends freely, who conducts his affairs with justice. 6 Surely he will never be shaken; a righteous man will be remembered forever. 7 He will have no fear of bad news; his heart is steadfast, trusting in the LORD. 8 His heart is secure, he will have no fear; in the end he will look in triumph on his foes. 9 He has scattered abroad his gifts to the poor, his righteousness endures forever; his horn will be lifted high in honor. 10 The wicked man will see and be vexed, he will gnash his teeth and waste away; the longings of the wicked will come to nothing.

Psalm 44 (New International Version)

For the director of music. Of the Sons of Korah. A "maskil."
1 We have heard with our ears, O God; our fathers have told us what you did in their days, in days long ago. 2 With your hand you drove out the nations and planted our fathers; you crushed the peoples and made our fathers flourish. 3 It was not by their sword that they won the land, nor did their arm bring them victory; it was your right hand, your arm, and the light of your face, for you loved them. 4 You are my King and my God, who decrees victories for Jacob. 5 Through you we push back our enemies; through your name we trample our foes. 6 I do not trust in my bow, my sword does not bring me victory; 7 but you give us victory over our enemies, you put our adversaries to shame. 8 In God we make our boast all day long, and we will praise your name forever. "Selah" 9But now you

have rejected and humbled us; you no longer go out with our armies. 10 You made us retreat before the enemy, and our adversaries have plundered us. 11 You gave us up to be devoured like sheep and have scattered us among the nations. 12 You sold your people for a pittance, gaining nothing from their sale. 13 You have made us a reproach to our neighbors, the scorn and derision of those around us. 14 You have made us a byword among the nations; the peoples shake their heads at us. 15 My disgrace is before me all day long, and my face is covered with shame 16 at the taunts of those who reproach and revile me, because of the enemy, who is bent on revenge. 17 All this happened to us, though we had not forgotten you or been false to your covenant. 18 Our hearts had not turned back; our feet had not strayed from your path. 19 But you crushed us and made us a haunt for jackals and covered us over with deep darkness. 20 If we had forgotten the name of our God or spread out our hands to a foreign god, 21 would not God have discovered it, since he knows the secrets of the heart? 22 Yet for your sake we face death all day long; we are considered as sheep to be slaughtered. 23 Awake, O Lord! Why do you sleep? Rouse yourself ! Do not reject us forever. 24 Why do you hide your face and forget our misery and oppression? 25 We are brought down to the dust; our bodies cling to the ground. 26 Rise up and help us; redeem us because of your unfailing love.

Psalm 25 (New International Version)

Of David.
1 To you, O LORD, I lift up my soul; 2 in you I trust, O my God. Do not let me be put to shame, nor let my enemies triumph over me. 3 No one whose hope is in you will ever be put to shame, but they will be

put to shame who are treacherous without excuse. 4 Show me your ways, O LORD, teach me your paths; 5 guide me in your truth and teach me, for you are God my Savior, and my hope is in you all day long. 6 Remember, O LORD, your great mercy and love, for they are from of old. 7Remember not the sins of my youth and my rebellious ways; according to your love remember me, for you are good, O LORD. 8 Good and upright is the LORD; therefore he instructs sinners in his ways. 9 He guides the humble in what is right and teaches them his way. 10 All the ways of the LORD are loving and faithful for those who keep the demands of his covenant. 11 For the sake of your name, O LORD, forgive my iniquity, though it is great. 12 Who, then, is the man that fears the LORD? He will instruct him in the way chosen for him. 13 He will spend his days in prosperity, and his descendants will inherit the land. 14 The LORD confides in those who fear him; he makes his covenant known to them. 15 My eyes are ever on the LORD, for only he will release my feet from the snare. 16 Turn to me and be gracious to me, for I am lonely and afflicted. 17 The troubles of my heart have multiplied; free me from my anguish. 18 Look upon my affliction and my distress and take away all my sins. 19 See how my enemies have increased and how fiercely they hate me! 20 Guard my life and rescue me; let me not be put to shame, for I take refuge in you. 21 May integrity and uprightness protect me, because my hope is in you. 22 Redeem Israel, O God, from all their troubles!

The Will of God lies in this: to love the people without expecting them to love you in return.
Beinsa Duno

Table of Contents

1. The master Beinsa Duno about prayer 4
2. The Lord's Prayer 14
3. The Good Prayer 15
4. Psalm 91 18
5. Prayer of the Path of Life 19
6. Prayer of the Spirit 21
7. Prayer of the Holy Spirit 25
8. Prayer of the Kingdom 26
9. Prayer the Fruits of the Spirit ... 28
10. Prayer of the Triune God 29
11. Prayer of Sacred Purity 31
12. The Small Prayer 33
13. Prayer of Gratitude 33
14. Prayer of the Chosen Ones 35
15. Blessing the Bulgarian Nation . 36
16. The New Credo 37
17. Prayer for Personal Uplifting ... 38
18. Prayer my Belief 38
19. Prayer for Full Success of the Cause 39
20. Praise to the King of All Ages .. 40

21. Prayer of Daniel 43
22. Prayer when in difficulty 44
23. Prayer 45
24. Morning Prayer of the Disciple . 46
25. Morning Prayer 47
26. Morning Prayer 48
27. Morning Prayer 48
28. Morning Prayer 49
29. Morning Prayer 50
30. Morning Prayer 50
31. Morning Prayer 51
32. Prayer on Awakening 51
33. Evening Prayer 52
34. Evening Prayer 52
35. Evening Prayer 53
36. Evening Prayer 53
37. Prayer for Every Day 54
38. Prayer for Protection in Thunderstorms and Earthquakes 55
39. Prayer for Rain 56
40. Prayer of the Spirit of the Solid Foundation 58
41. Prayer of the Disciple of the Brotherhood of Light 58

42. Prayer of the Disciple 59
43. Prayer of the Disciple 60
44. Prayer of the Disciple 60
45. Prayer of the Disciple 61
46. The Good Path 61
47. Prayer to the Spirit of Truth 63
48. The Beautiful Prayer 63
49. Prayer in Sanskrit 65
50. Prayer for Healing 65
51. Prayer for Healing 66
52. Prayer for Healing 66
53. Prayer for Health 67
54. Prayer for 10 Day Fasting 67
55. Prayer for Healing of Another Person 68
56. Prayer for Healing of Another Person 69
57. Prayer Before and After Meals .. 70
58. Prayer Before and After Meals .. 70
59. Prayer Before Meal 71
60. Prayer After Meal 71
61. Prayer Before Meal 71
62. Prayer Before Meal 72
63. Prayer Before Meal 72

64. Lozinka 72
65. Lozinka 75
66. Prayers for the Departed 78
67. Prayer for the Departed Souls .. 79
68. Prayer for the Departed Souls .. 80
69. Secret Prayer 81
70. The Lord's Prayer 81
71. Psalm 23 82
72. Psalm 121 83
73. Prayer of Daniel 84
74. John 14:1-7 85
75. Formulas 86
76. Prayer 86
77. Prayer for Blessing 87
78. Agnus Dei 88
79. The Wellspring of Good 89
80. Prayer of the Mission of the Master 90
81. Prayer 93
82. Short Prayers 94
83. Prayer 94
84. Prayer 95
85. Prayer 95
86. Prayer 96

87. Prayer	....	96
88. Prayer	....	97
89. Prayer	....	98
90. Prayer	....	98
91. Prayer	....	99
92. Prayer	....	99
93. Prayer	....	100
94. Prayer	....	100
95. Prayer	....	101
96. Prayer	....	101
97. Prayer	....	102
98. Prayer	....	102
99. Prayer	....	103
100. Prayer	....	103
101. Prayer	....	104
102. Prayer	....	105
103. Prayer	....	105
104. Prayer	....	106
105. The Lovely Prayer of the Mother	....	107
106. Motto-Prayer	....	107
107. FORMULAS	....	108
108. Formulas for Protection	....	109
109. Morning Formulas	....	120

110. Formulas for Deep Breathing 134
111. Formula Before Meal 140
112. Formulas for Healing 140
113. Commandment of the Master 157
114. Greeting 162
115. The Sacred Formula 163
116. Formulas When in Difficulty .. 175
117. The Priceless Formula 176
118. Evening Formulas 189
119. Psalm 91 191
120. Psalm 23 193
121. Psalm 133 194
122. Psalm 117 194
123. Psalm 121 195
124. Psalm 61 195
125. Psalm 143 196
126. Psalm 27 198
127. Psalm 19 200
128. Psalm 103 201
129. Psalm 112 203
130. Psalm 44 205
131. Psalm 25 207

Made in the USA
Columbia, SC
02 January 2019